The Amazing Mullet

How To Catch, Smoke And Cook The Fish

Adam Marianski

Bookmagic LLC,
Seminole, Florida

Copyright © 2011 by Bookmagic, LLC.

All rights reserved. This book may not be reproduced in any manner without the express written consent of the publisher, except of brief quotations in critical reviews and articles.

The Amazing Mullet How To Catch, Smoke And Cook The Fish
Adam Marianski

Cover photo courtesy Benjamin Cox, Original, North Carolina.

ISBN: 978-0-9824267-8-4
Library of Congress Control Number: 2011909181

Bookmagic, LLC.
http://www.bookmagic.com

Printed in the United States of America.

Contents

	Introduction	5
Chapter 1	**The Amazing Mullet**	7
Chapter 2	**Catching Mullet**	13
	Cast Nets	14
	Cast Net Sizes	17
	Learn Your Area	22
	Net Casting From a Boat	24
	Additional Equipment	24
	Learning to Cast a Net	24
Chapter 3	**Safety Considerations**	29
	Salting	29
	Smoking	30
	Cooking	30
	Freezing and Thawing	30
	Cleanliness and Common Sense	31
Chapter 4	**Cleaning Mullet**	35
	Dressing Mullet "Butterfly" Style	36
	Dressing Whole Mullet	42
	Processing a Large Mullet Catch	46
	Filleting	49
	Cleaning Fish Without Cutting	51
	Bleeding Fish	52

Chapter 5   **Brining Mullet** 53

    Making Brine 55
    Brining Times 58
    Influence of Salt on Fish Presentation 59
    What's Better Dry Salting or Brine 59
    More About Salt 60

Chapter 6   **Smoking Mullet** 61

    Smoking - Reasons 61
    What is Smoking 62
    Cold Smoking 63
    Hot Smoking 63
    Wood For Smoking 67
    Fish Flesh Color 67
    Smoking Mullet 68
    Hanging/Drying Fish 69
    Pellicle 70
    Cooking Temperature 76
    Cooling 76
    Storing 76
    Smokers 76

Chapter 7   **Cooking Mullet** 81

    Recipes 84
    Spreads 93
    Sauces 98
    Roe 113

    Index 117

Introduction

Mullet is an amazing fish that is being overlooked. Most of us are fascinated by the little jumping fish that we know nothing about. There are some that have never seen it. Yet the fish is present in every little bay, bayou or canal as long as there is a warm water connecting to the ocean. If you see a silvery fish jumping out of the water, you have met the mullet. This fish is absolutely wonderful when smoked but can be prepared by any cooking method. Catching mullet offers a challenge as the fish avoids the common fishing rod and lure. You have to learn the art of casting a net, then there is no limit to what you can bring home.

I would like to give special thanks to Roger Edwards who has introduced me to the art of catching mullet. Without his extensive knowledge, this book would not have been written.

Adam Marianski

Chapter 1

All About Mullet

The mullet is a very unique fish. It is a schooling fish that can withstand a wide range of saline levels. Mullet feed on algae, plankton and detritus (disintegrated matter). These characteristics allow mullet to thrive in saltwater, brackish water, and freshwater. They tend to inhabit shallow, warm coastal waters throughout many countries.

Mullet are a species of fish from the Mugilidae family. The family includes about 80 species in 17 genera, although half of the species are in just two genera (Liza and Mugil). There are two common types of mullet found throughout the Gulf of Mexico. The silver mullet and the striped mullet. The striped mullet is a larger fish ranging from around 1 to 2 feet and the silver mullet measures up to one foot.

Different species have distinct features, for example Indian Ocean mullet are red in color. The red mullet are also common in the Mediterranean Region. They are a small bottom-feeding fish with different distinguishing characteristics than the American mullet. This book is about the wonderful American mullet, which when smoked is only second to salmon. Even though mullet is so widely distributed, there are many who have never seen or heard of the fish. This can be attributed to a few reasons:

- Mullet inhibit shallow waters such as bays, lagoons, bayous, generally speaking the sheltered waters. This effectively protects mullet from commercial vessels and from being processed on a large commercial scale.
- Mullet like warm waters, 70-90° F (21-32° C). People living in tropical areas are familiar with silver or striped mullet, but those living in cooler climates have not seen them.
- Mullet are vegetarians that eat detritus, which is disintegrated material found at the bottom. It is almost futile to catch mullet with a fishing rod. To catch mullet you need a cast net and many states do not permit its use.

Photo 1.1 Striped mullet.

Photo 1.2 Silver mullet.

Mullet have no teeth and they suck in food from the muddy bottom. What makes mullet unique is that they have a gizzard (stomach) which holds indigestible material and breaks it down. A mullet gizzard is surprisingly similar to a chicken gizzard in taste, function, and appearance. It is a small round circle that is around one inch in diameter, depending on the size of the mullet. Many consider this a delicacy.

Photo 1.3 Mullet gizzards.

Mullet are a coastal species that have an affinity for tropical and warm temperate waters. Many consider the Gulf of Mexico to be mullet country, and of course they are everywhere in West Florida. However, they can be found throughout the entire east coast of the United States reaching Nova Scotia, Canada, and on the west coast of the United States from Southern California down to Chile, the coast of Brazil, the Mediterranean Sea, the Black Sea, the coast of France, around the entire coast of Africa, Taiwan, and in Australia. As the water temperature rises in the summer months, mullet wander into and are more abundant in brackish and freshwater. Mullet are able to tolerate wide salinity and temperature levels of water and those characteristics allow the fish to prosper in many areas of the world. Mullet reproduce in the winter months from October through December, which is known as roe season. They migrate offshore to deeper water where they spawn. In the Gulf of Mexico mullet have been observed spawning 40-50 miles offshore. A single mullet is capable of producing from 0.5 million to 2.0 million eggs. The females lay spherical shaped transparent eggs containing oil globules. These globules provide the egg with a positive buoyancy, keeping it from sinking to the bottom. Once a female lays its eggs, they hatch about 48 hours later producing larvae that are around 2.4 mm in length. When these larvae grow to 16-20 mm, they make their way back inshore to very shallow water. They can be found along any shore whether it be a seawall, rock jetty, oyster beds, mangroves, as long as it is around 1 to 2 foot deep water. They remain in this water where there is plenty of food while they are protected from predators. When they grow to about 2 to 3 inches in length, they are commonly known as "finger mullet." Finger mullet are an excellent bait to use and you can catch just about any fish with them.

Many fishermen look forward to fishing for mullet during roe season. During this time of year mullet are highly sought after for the added bonus of their roe. The fish eggs found in female mullet and the sperm found in male mullet during the spawning season are referred to as roe. In a male the roe is white in color and in a female the roe is yellow.

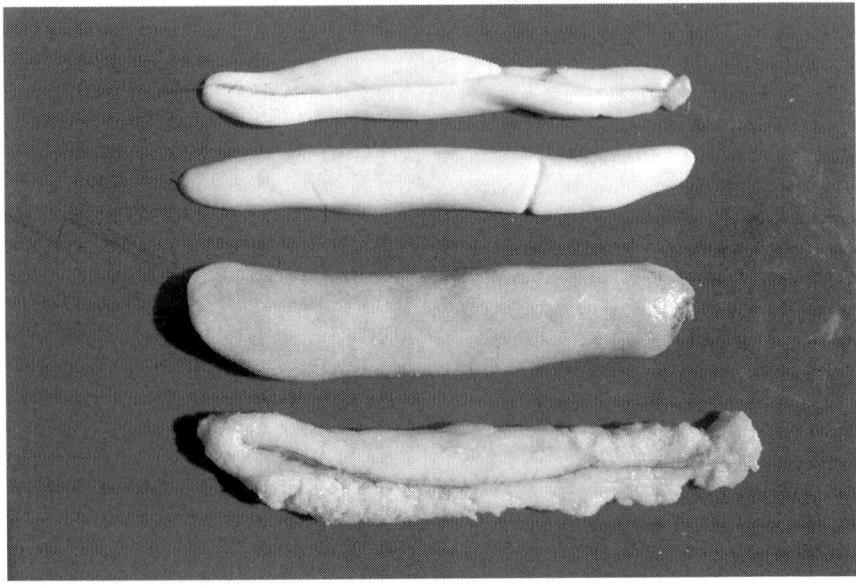

Photo 1.4 Mullet roe and sperm. Roe is often scrambled and fried like eggs. Large quantities of roe are exported every year to Japan.

Chapter 1 - All About Mullet

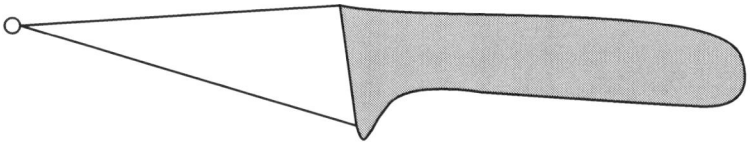

Fig 1.1 Mullet roe knife. The ball at the end of the knife prevents the knife from cutting the roe.

A male's roe, which is also known as milt, is not as sought after like a female's roe. Yellow roe is excellent smoked or fried. The roe can reach eight inches in length and weigh up to 0.75 pounds, varying according to the size of the mullet. Roe is considered a delicacy and can yield a high price in fish markets. A significant amount of roe is exported every year to Japan. There are many recipes and methods of cooking with mullet roe.

Mullet are a schooling fish. They tend to school in shallower waters with sandy or muddy bottoms and in heavily vegetated areas. They are plentiful near grass flats and can be seen jumping out of the water in succession. Every fisherman has asked the question before, "Why do mullet jump out of the water like that?" Only a mullet knows for sure and we can only speculate as to the possible reasons.

Photo 1.5 Mullet jumping out of the water.

Photo courtesy Benjamin Cox, Oriental, North Carolina.

It is a subject that is always brought up and most people believe they do it to avoid predators. Here are the most probable reasons that cause mullet to jump out of the water:

- The first and simplest reason is to avoid predators. Most people think this is the only reason, however, studies prove else wise.
- Mullet are common to many parasites. Some fish rub against structure such as rocks, pilings, or the sea floor. Mullet leap out of the water and as they land and make contact with the water they are able to shake off some of those parasites that are attached to their bodies.

We know that fish use their gills to breathe. However, they do not breathe and process water. They breathe the dissolved oxygen found in water. Knowing this we have to take into account that plants use dissolved oxygen as well. Plants are commonly known to use carbon dioxide and produce oxygen through photosynthesis. However, it is not a well known fact that at night and on cloudy days, without sunlight present, photosynthesis does not take place and these submerged plants and algae use oxygen from the water for respiration. This lowers the dissolved oxygen content of water leaving less for mullet to intake. Mullet are bottom feeders and basically sift through debris to eat. Additionally mullet thrive in tropical waters, warm water is less able to hold dissolved gasses than colder water, further lowering the oxygen content. They spend much time in murky water near grass flats or areas with sandy or muddy bottoms. All these factors combined cause mullet to leap out of the water to replenish their gills with fresh, clean air.

In his famous song "Summertime" George Gershwin mentions mullet:

"Summertime, and the living is easy, fish are jumping and the cotton is high..."

Yes, in those days there were many cotton plantations and a lot of mullet jumping in Southern Gulf states and in Georgia. There are less cotton plantations today, but mullets keep on jumping.

Chapter 2

Catching Mullet

The fact that a mullet is a vegetarian brings up an issue of how to catch them. What kind of bait do you use to catch a fish that eats algae and tiny disintegrated matter? Well most saltwater fishermen will tell you that it is not possible to catch a mullet with a rod and reel. However, this is not entirely true. In marine water it is rare, but when a mullet ventures into brackish water, a freshwater stream or lake and becomes acclimated to that environment, its eating behavior slightly changes. In freshwater and brackish water it is possible to catch mullet with a rod and reel using earthworms, chicken feed, oats, or bread for bait. However, it is not commonly practiced as many consider it a futile task. Cast netting is a common and widely practiced method to catching mullet. They are a schooling fish and it is common to catch several dozen at a time with a cast net.

They can be caught at any time, day or night, and in various locations as well. They are found inshore from a boat, grassflats, piers, off seawalls, docks, bridges, canals, and streams. Their abundance near all these areas is appealing as a fisherman can catch them practically anywhere. Mullet are especially attractive to many because a boat is not needed to catch them. Another advantage is that typical fishing restrictions that usually limit fish quota to a few fish per person, do not apply to mullet.

Large schools of mullet frequently swim near the surface in shallow waters making them an easy target. With the use of a cast net, it is common for a fisherman to catch 10 to 20 mullet in one throw. Sometimes you only catch 2 or 5, and sometimes you can catch 40 or 50. It just depends on how thick the mullet are schooling. In the state of Florida an individual is allowed to catch and keep 50 mullet per day and this is a lot of food on the table. There are no size limitations or restrictions. Laws may vary so it is a good idea to check with your local fish and game authority.

In the past fishermen used a primitive method of catching mullet called "snatching." Snatch, treble or quad hooks were attached to a line on a long pole. A fisherman would hold the pole and lower the hooks into the water keeping them suspended a few inches off the bottom. When a school of fish would swim through, the fisherman would jerk the pole upward in hopes of snatching a fish with the hook. This is rather a cruel method and is outlawed in many places, for example in Australia, where it is known as "jagging".

Cast Nets

A cast net is a circular shaped mesh net with weights evenly distributed along its outer perimeter. When the net is thrown or "cast" it opens out and lands over the fish trapping them underneath. It looks like a parachute or the top of an umbrella falling down.

Photo 2.1 Cast net falling down. In time you will be able to control how far and where to send the net.

Cast nets have been around forever. There have been many advancements made to cast nets throughout history. Early cast nets were nothing more than a circular net with weights attached around the perimeter. Once thrown, a fisherman would have to find the net and carefully remove the fish one by one. Fortunately the modern day cast net has a hand line which allows the fisherman to pull the net to him. This advancement allows the fisherman to throw in much deeper water while ensuring he will not lose fish once they are caught.

Chapter 2 - Catching Mullet

There are various styles and sizes of cast nets that can be used but all modern cast nets are composed of the following parts:

- Hand line - a braided polyethylene line, floats in the water, has a loop on the end that attaches to the thrower's wrist.

- Brail lines - monofilaments lines that connect hand line to the lead line (perimeter of the net). The connection is made by means of a swivel which prevents any entanglement of brail lines with the hand line. These brail lines go through a center ring or "horn" and attach in designated places to the lead line.

- Horn – plastic ring where the net is attached to, the horn allows the brail lines to pass through and connect (through the swivel) to the hand line enabling a thrower to open and close the net.

- Lead line – braided polyethylene line that is the perimeter of the net when open. The weights or leads are attached and evenly spaced on the lead line. The lead line can be considered the outer perimeter of the cast net.

- Mesh size – monofilament line intertwined to make even openings that are consistent throughout the net.

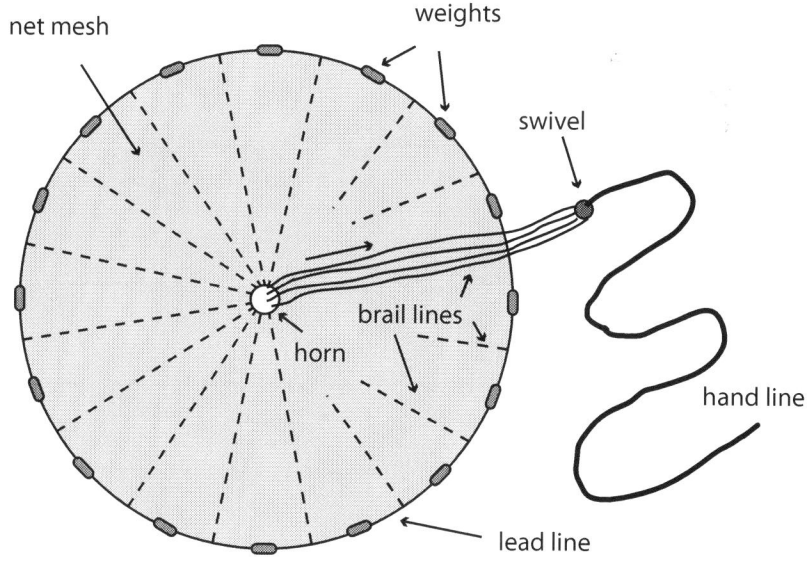

Fig 2.1 Cast net.

When the net is cast the weighted lead line pulls the brail lines through the center of the horn to the bottom.

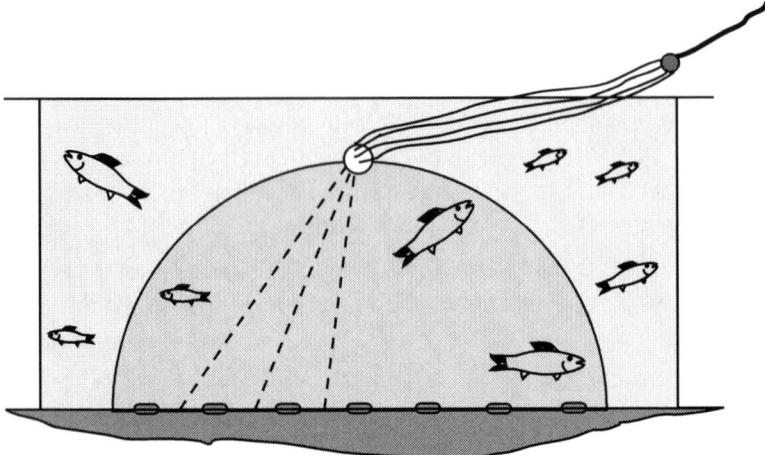

Fig 2.2 Cast net is thrown and sinks to the bottom.

To retrieve the net and the fish, the thrower pulls out the hand line. The hand line pulls the brail lines up and closes the outer perimeter of the net. This creates a round bag which holds the fish. Once when the entire hand line is retrieved, the thrower grabs the brail lines and pulls them and the closed net up.

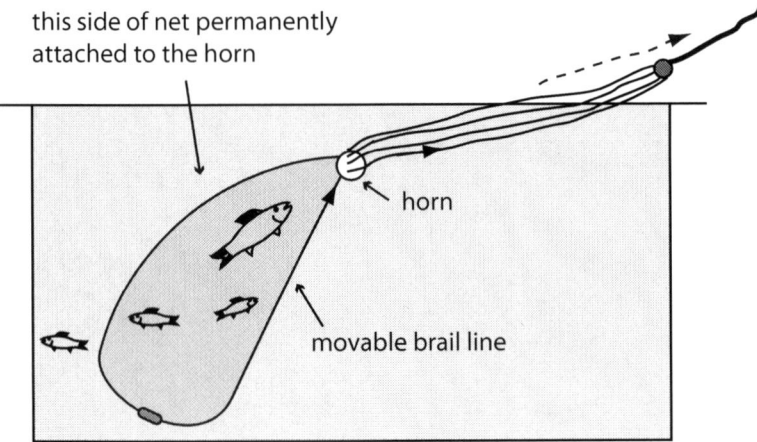

Fig 2.3 Retrieving the net.

Chapter 2 - Catching Mullet

Once the net is landed, the horn is pulled up and the brail lines are drawn back through the horn. This opens the net (the bag disappears) and the fish are able to be removed.

Cast Net Sizes

In the state of Florida, the largest size net that a fisherman can legally use is a 14' net. This is measured from the horn to the lead line, which is the radius of the net. So when the net is thrown into the water, it will have an outside perimeter that is 28' in diameter. When selecting a cast net, there are several factors that must be taken into account. You must decide on a mesh size, the weight of the net, the size of the net when opened, and the material the net is made of. The mesh size varies widely for each individual's preference. It depends on what type and size of fish you are targeting. While a net with a larger mesh size like 2.5 inches will not catch smaller fish, a net with a mesh size of 1 inch will catch larger and smaller fish. A net with a larger mesh size will sink faster than a net with the same size weights that has a smaller mesh size.

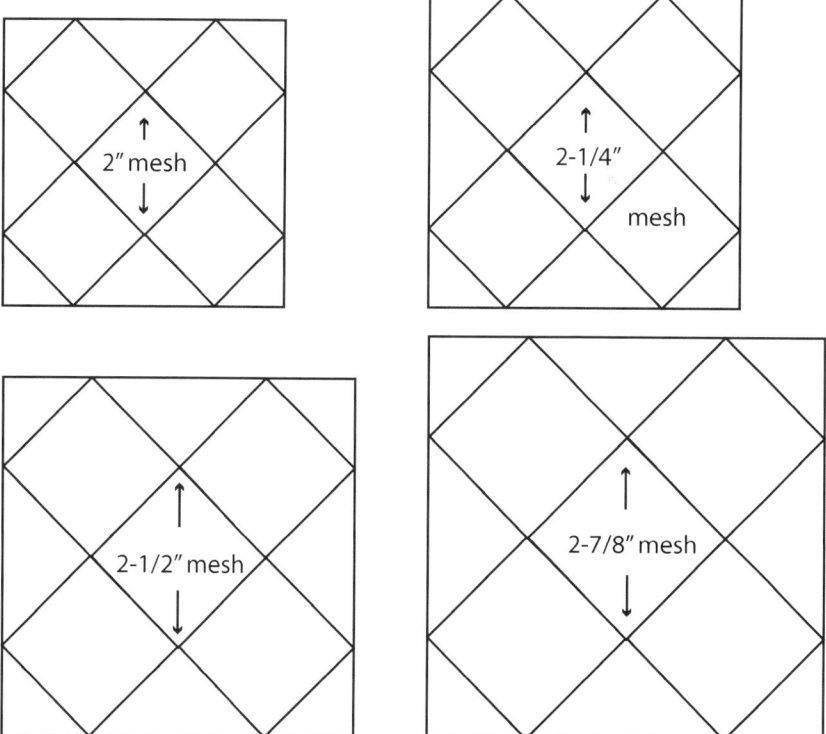

Fig 2.4 Net mesh popular sizes.

Mesh suggested uses:
- 1" - small silver mullet and larger fish.
- 1-1/2" - large silver mullet and larger fish.
- 2" - striped mullet, sheepshead, other large fish.
- 2-1/4" - large striped mullet, sheepshead, other large fish.

The net with a small mesh size has more lines intertwined creating more resistance in the water. A one inch mullet net with one ounce weights is ideal to catch all mullet as it will only let the smallest of fish escape through the mesh. The one ounce weights will suffice to let the net sink fast enough. If someone is fit they can get a net with heavier weights, however, this may prevent the fisherman from throwing the net many times as he may tire sooner.

Cast nets come in many sizes from 5 feet to 14 foot. Keep in mind that a *14' net thrown will form a 28' diameter circle*. It is easier to learn net throwing with a smaller net, let's say 8 or 10 foot as it is lighter and requires less folding. Most of my friends, myself included, carry a 12 foot net.

Casting a net is not fishing, it is an art.

Chapter 2 - Catching Mullet

Fig 2.3 With a bit of practice you will make each throw a perfect one.

Most of today's cast nets are made of monofilament line. This is the same as the fishing line found on a fishing reel. Monofilament is extremely popular because of its ability to cut through water and sink quickly, while weighing next to nothing. When removed from water, the line is almost instantly dry absorbing practically none of the water. Some cast nets are made from green monofilament line as it reflects less light, increasing your chances of catching fish.

It has been learned that fish have very good eyesight, with mullet not being an exception. It is common for a school of mullet to swim towards a fisherman and when that fisherman attempts to throw a cast net, the fish dart away. This is commonly referred to as starbursting. Sometimes they notice the individual's movement, sometimes they see the net coming towards the water, and sometimes they see the individual's shadow move. Monofilament line can reflect light which will startle the mullet and frighten them.

Many fishermen fish for mullet at night to decrease the chances of being spotted by fish. When fishing at night it is advised to wear dark clothes as it is easier for the fish to spot a white shirt in the dark. It is also believed that as a fish is approaching and it sees a white outline in the distance, it is frightened and thinks that outline is the underbelly of a dolphin or a larger fish that may pose a threat.

Fish are easily spooked and if fishing in crystal clear conditions, there is a good chance that the fish will see you. When fishing in murky water they have a more difficult time seeing you, but at the same time you may have trouble spotting them at first. Once you get accustomed to their appearance in the water you will catch them with ease. When you throw the net over a school of mullet be sure to *let it sink to the bottom before you attempt to pull it in.* If you get excited and start pulling the hand line too soon, mullet may still be able to swim underneath the lead line and escape. When your net sinks to the bottom, begin pulling the hand line in by slowly tugging it while holding it as low to the ground as possible. This is done as a safety precaution to ensure that the net will not lift up off the bottom. If casting on a sandy bottom with good visibility, you can see the difference in how the net closes using this method or if you just pull it in. After the lead line comes together and the net closes, you can pull as hard and fast as you want. The fish are trapped inside.

When fishing from a seawall, dock, or bridge, be cautious pulling the net in once it gets close to you. It is very important to lean forward and pull the net out of the water as fast as possible to keep it from touching the structure that you are fishing from. Pilings and seawalls are usually covered in oysters or barnacles and it is easy for your mesh to get caught and stuck. If your net gets snagged on an obstruction and you pull hard enough, it is possible that you will tear the mesh.

Cast nets are most commonly stored and carried in five gallon buckets. Keeping your net in these buckets is extremely convenient as any size net will fit comfortably inside. It also provides for an easy way to move around and carry the net to and from different locations.

Photo 2.4 Folding cast net.

Photo 2.5 Folded net in a storage bucket.

It is recommended to clean your net as frequently as possible. Just like any other equipment, if you keep it nice and clean, it will last longer.

A popular method used to clean a net is to set it in a five gallon bucket, fill it with water and add about one cup of fabric softener. This method is commonly practiced as it softens the monofilament. When a net has not been cleaned for some time, the monofilament will become tough and less flexible.

The net does not discriminate against the fish below and what you sometimes catch may surprise you:

Photo 2.6 Adam with a large jack crevalle.

With a cast net it is common to catch fish like: sheepshead, snappers, red fish, jacks, flounder, tilapia, lady fish, mackerel and others. Be familiar with the local fishing regulations as *not all fish are allowed to be caught with a net*. Once when mastered net casting is a very effective method of catching a variety of fish. Keep in mind that many states do not allow it, so do your homework.

Photo 2.7 Typical size jacks caught with a net.

Learn Your Area

It is important to be aware of your surroundings. Get to know what the bottom looks like and throw the net in areas that you are familiar with. A good idea is to check out the area in the daytime first before fishing it at night. There is nothing worse than getting a net hung up on a piling, tree branches, mangroves, oyster beds, or rocks. All these can tear your net or possibly force you to part with it. If there are obstructions in the water, the mesh may get caught in them when you are pulling the net.

Photo 2.8 Numerous bayous are filled with mullet. When throwing in unknown territory, be prepared to get in the water and free the net if it gets stuck. And wear some old sneakers for protection, unless you want to be rushed to the nearest hospital.

As you start throwing a net you will find out from your friends and your own experience which areas are best to catch mullet. Mullet are everywhere, but as you have learnt so far, in order not to lose your rather expensive net, you have to fish in areas which offer no obstructions. You need to have a strong footing as you may have to pull a 100 lb load out of the water. For all those above reasons it comes as no surprise that the most popular locations are little bridges, piers and concrete seawalls. Dozens of bridges stand over canals that connect coastal communities in Florida and schools of mullet swim in those water channels. Nets can be cast directly over the railing of the bridge or from the concrete seawall.

Chapter 2 - Catching Mullet 23

Photo 2.9 Coffee Pot Boulevard, St.Petersburg, Florida, is one of the favorite places for catching mullet as there are numerous concrete seawalls around. Snell Isle Bridge in the background.

Photo 2.10 Cast netting from a dock.

Net Casting From a Boat

A flat bottom fishing boat with a steady deck is a fantastic tool to have when fishing. With a boat you don't need to wait for the schools to swim by, you can follow and find them. As you will be chasing mullet and getting close to them, an electric trolling motor is beneficial as it operates silently. This is a two man operation, one person controls the boat while another is standing on the deck ready to throw the net. At the present writing the use of gill nets is not allowed. There is some poaching present and moonlight operators can harvest thousands of pounds of mullet in one night, but when caught they go to jail.

Additional Equipment

Besides a five gallon bucket and the net you need a cooler filled with ice. When cast netting you should always be prepared to catch many fish, as it happens quite frequently. Polarized glasses are an essential tool in any kind of fishing during the day. They block the reflection of sunlight from the surface of the water eliminating much of the glare. This makes the water more transparent to the human eye enabling a fisherman to see deeper and clearer into the water.

Learning to Cast a Net

Cast nets come with instructions so this is your starting point. You can also buy videos on the subject or learn it from a friend. In addition, there are many free video clips on the Internet at www.youtube.com and other sites.

A word of advice is to:

- Practice in your back yard first and then go out and catch mullet.
- You will be most successful throwing a cast net in areas without any obstructions.

Photo 2.12 Stretch the cast net out in order to fold it properly. Loop the handline and hold it in your right hand.

Photo 2.13 Grab the net with both hands as shown. Continue holding the handline.

Photo 2.14 Fold the net over and hold both places with your right hand, continuing to hold the handline.

Photo 2.15 Raise into the air to grab the lead line.

Photo 2.16 Once you grab the lead line, set the net down and place the lead line in your mouth.

Photo 2.17 Next with your left arm stretch the net to the side to begin separating it.

Photo 2.18 Lift the net and with your left arm swing the leads around your shoulder.

Photo 2.19 Continue swinging until you have the leads separated about half way.

Photo 2.20 Set the net down and grab the net with your left hand as shown. Right hand has been holding the same position since the beginning.

Photo 2.21 Pick net up and get in position to throw.

Chapter 2 - Catching Mullet

Photo 2.23 Release net with both hands at same time.

Photo 2.22 Position net behind you to increase momentum and swing in one motion.

Anatomy of a Throw

Photo 2.12 Releasing net.

Photo 2.13 Fully released.

Photo 2.14 Spreading open.

Photo 2.15 Fully open.

Photo 2.16 Landed.

Chapter 3

Safety Considerations

The flesh of a healthy fish is clean and contains very few bacteria. Any invading bacteria will be destroyed by the fish's immune system and as long as fish remain alive, they are healthy. Most of the bacteria in fish is present in the slime that covers its body and in its digestive tract. Removing fish from its natural environment, freshwater or saltwater, creates favorable conditions for bacteria to multiply. Every time a knife cuts meat, the blade introduces new bacteria which multiply and slowly migrate towards the inside of the piece. Some bacteria are present on our hands while others live in our nose and throat, so personal hygiene is of utmost importance as well.

There are two reasons that fish spoils faster than other meat:

1. Its meat contains more water (bacteria need moisture)

> Beef - 60% water
> Veal, poultry - 66% water
> Lean fish - 70% water
> Fat fish - 80% water

2. Its meat contains very little salt (salt inhibits the growth of bacteria). Both freshwater and saltwater fish have a very low salt content in their meat (0.2-0.7% of salt). When salt is applied to fish, it removes water from the meat which inhibits the growth of bacteria.

Salting is one of the oldest methods of food preservation. Heavy salting of fish is practiced today only in undeveloped nations but in the past it was commonly used to preserve and transport fish to different countries. To stop bacteria from growing by salt alone, the salt levels would be so high that the product will not be edible in its original state. It would have to be soaked in water first to eliminate the excess salt and only then it could be cooked.

Smoking fish has been practiced as a preservation technique before man realized its added benefit to taste. Smoking imparts a different flavor, fights bacteria, especially on the surface of the product, and thus to a certain degree prevents the growth of microorganisms in fish. Keep in mind that only prolonged cold smoking can be thought of as a preservation method. Products that are cold smoked contain much higher levels of salt which prevent bacteria growth in the first stages of smoking. We usually don't practice cold smoking fish anymore, cold smoked salmon (lox) being the exception.

Fish contains about 70-80% water and this moisture is the main reason that it spoils. Think of it as a community pool and if the weather is warm, all bacteria types go swimming. Given favorable conditions they can double up in numbers every 20 minutes. In a refrigerator their number will also grow, albeit at a reduced pace, but they can double up in 12 hours. Short of deep freezing, it is impossible to stop bacteria from contaminating meat, but we can create conditions that will slow down their growth rate. At room temperatures bacteria will grow anywhere they have access to nutrients and water. The easiest methods that we can apply to preserve fish are to:

- Keep it alive as long as possible. This is accomplished by holding fish in cages hooked up to the boat or holding fish in tanks. In underdeveloped countries people keep fish alive in any suitable containers. When the war ended in Europe, there were no refrigerators around and keeping fish for a few days in a bathtub was a common practice. Such preservation methods, which lasted only a few days, functioned quite well.

- Lower the temperature. This is simply done by refrigerating or keeping fish on ice. Any fish processed outside should be kept in an ice filled container.

Cooking Fish

Fish is considered done when cooked to 145° F (63° C) internal temperature. A reliable test is to insert a fork or knife into the thickest part of the fish and twist. The flesh should flake (separate).

Freezing and Thawing

Fresh fish should not be kept in a refrigerator for more than a few days. Smoked fish will last up to a week. For longer storage time, all fish must

Chapter 3 - Safety Considerations

be frozen. Keep in mind that during freezing water increases in volume and forms crystals. Those crystals will inflict some damage to the internal structure of the fish and its texture will never be as firm again. This will be less pronounced in cases of smoked and cooked fish as a significant amount of moisture was removed during processing and less ice crystals will form during freezing. Thawing is a much slower process than freezing and is usually done in a refrigerator. The process would be faster if performed at a higher temperature, but that would create favorable conditions for the growth of bacteria. During thawing a liquid leaks out from the meat/fish being thawed. This liquid is the result of ruptured meat cells and connective tissues by ice crystals. It is the combination of extracted meat proteins, meat juice, minerals, blood, water and other components.

Fish and meats should be thawed by one of the following methods:

- Refrigerator. The air exhibits very poor conductivity and the thawing process is slow.
- Water. Water transfers heat or cold much better than air and the fish immersed in ice cold water (plastic bag is used) will thaw out much faster.
- Microwave. Make sure that fish cuts are of uniform size.

Cleanliness and Common Sense

Home made fish are subject to the ambient temperature of the kitchen and a dose of a common sense is of invaluable help:

- Take only what you need from the cooler.
- When a fish has been processed put it back into the cooler.
- Keep your equipment clean and cold.
- Work as fast as possible.
- Try to always keep meat/fish refrigerated.
- If your premises are not temperature controlled, limit your production to late evening or early morning hours.
- Wash your hands often.
- Be aware of the "danger zone" (40-140° F, 4-60° C).

All bacteria need moisture, nutrients, and warm temperatures to grow. Bacteria love water and temperatures that revolve around the temperature of our body (98.6° F, 36.6° C). Holding products at higher temperatures (greater than 130° F, 54° C) restricts the growth of bacteria. Increasing temperatures over 140° F (60° C) will start killing them. Most bacteria need oxygen (aerobic), others thrive without it (anaerobic). All of them hate cold and at around 32° F, (0° C) they become lethargic and when the temperature drops even lower, they become dormant. *Keeping them at low temperatures does not kill them, but only stops them from multiplying.* Once when the conditions are favorable again, they will wake up and start growing again.

There are bacteria (e.g. *Clostridium botulinum*) that are able to survive high temperatures because they form spores. Spores are special cells that envelop themselves in a protective shell and become resistant to harsh environmental conditions. Once conditions become favorable, the cells return to their actively growing state.

Fish like any other meat is susceptible to food poisoning given the right conditions for the development of *C. Botulinum* spores into toxins. Those conditions (*lack of oxygen*, humidity, temperatures 40-140° F, 4-60° C) always exist when smoking meats. To eliminate the possibility of such a danger Cure # 1 is added the same way it is used when smoking meats or sausages. You will come across many recipes and some will call for adding Cure #1, and most will not. Adding Cure #1 to smoked sausages is widely practiced and required from commercial producers. Most people who smoke fish are not familiar with Cure #1 and don't use it.

In order to eliminate nitrites (Cure #1) the salt concentration in the water should be high enough to inhibit the growth of *C. botulinum*, without making the product too salty to eat. A minimum concentration of 3% is considered to be effective for hot smoked fish. For comparison in most smoked sausages the salt concentration is about 2%. Smoking and cooking temperatures should be kept above the "danger zone" (140° F, 60° C). People on a low salt diet who prefer low salt concentration would be safer to include nitrites in the brine. Keep in mind that *Clostridium botulinum* bacteria *hate* fresh air so make sure that you have a supply of fresh air and not just a perfectly tight smoker. Any opening at the bottom or lower part of a smoker will provide fresh air. I don't want to unnecessarily scare you as food poisoning cases are very rare, but unfortunately they share one common factor: they are all fatal.

Parasites

Fish such as cobia, cod, flounder, grouper, halibut, herring, jack, mackerel, **mullet**, pollock, perch, rockfish, salmon, seatrout, trout are known to carry parasites. Cooking fish eliminates the danger of contracting a parasite, but many fish are not cooked at all, for example cold smoked fish or known dishes such as sushi, sashimi or increasingly popular ceviche. Such fish should be frozen according to the USDA guidelines that follow below.

Food and Drug Administration, Fish and Fishery Products, Hazards and Controls Guidance, Fourth Edition-April 2011:

Chapter 5 - Parasites

Parasites (in the larval stage) consumed in uncooked, or undercooked, unfrozen seafood can present a human health hazard. Among parasites, the nematodes or roundworms (Anisakis spp., Pseudoterranova spp., Eustrongylides spp. and Gnathostoma spp.), cestodes or tapeworms (Diphyllobothrium spp.) and trematodes or flukes (Chlonorchis sinensis, Opisthorchis spp., Heterophyes spp., Metagonimus spp., Nanophyetes salminicola and Paragonimus spp.) are of most concern in seafood. Some products that have been implicated in human infection are: ceviche (fish and spices marinated in lime juice); lomi lomi (salmon marinated in lemon juice, onion and tomato); poisson cru (fish marinated in citrus juice, onion, tomato and coconut milk); herring roe; sashimi (slices of raw fish); sushi (pieces of raw fish with rice and other ingredients); green herring (lightly brined herring); drunken crabs (crabs marinated in wine and pepper); cold-smoked fish; and, undercooked grilled fish. A recent survey of U.S. gastroenterologists has confirmed that seafood-borne parasitic infections occur in the U.S. with sufficient frequency to make preventive controls necessary during the processing of parasite-containing species of fish that are intended for raw consumption.

Controlling Parasites

The process of heating raw fish sufficiently to kill bacterial pathogens is also sufficient to kill parasites. Guidance concerning cooking and pasteurizing to kill pathogens is provided in Chapters 16 and 17. Regulatory requirements for retorting (low acid canned foods) are contained in 21 CFR 113. This Guide does not provide further guidance on retorting. The effectiveness of freezing to kill parasites depends on several factors, including the temperature of the freezing process, the length of time needed to freeze the fish tissue, the length of time the fish is held frozen, the fat content of the fish, and the type of parasite present. The temperature of the freezing process, the length of time the fish is held frozen, and the type of parasite appear to be the most important factors. For example, tapeworms are more susceptible to freezing than are roundworms. Flukes appear to be more resistant than roundworms.

Freezing and storing at -4°F (-20°C) or below for 7 days (total time), or freezing at -31°F (-35°C) or below until solid and storing at -31°F (-35°C) or below for 15 hours, or freezing at -31°F (-35°C) or below until solid and storing at -4°F (-20°C) or below for 24 hours is sufficient to kill parasites. FDA's Food Code recommends these freezing conditions to retailers who provide fish intended for raw consumption.

Note: these conditions may not be suitable for freezing particularly large fish (e.g. thicker than six inches). The effectiveness of hydrostatic pressure in the elimination of parasites from fish flesh is being studied.

Brining and pickling may reduce the parasite hazard in a fish, but they do not eliminate it, nor do they minimize it to an acceptable level. Nematode larvae have been shown to survive 28 days in an 80° salinometer brine (21% salt by weight).

Fish that contain parasites in their flesh may also contain parasites within their egg skeins, but generally not within the eggs themselves. For this reason, eggs that have been removed from the skein and rinsed are not likely to contain parasites.

Trimming away the belly flaps of fish or candling and physically removing parasites are effective methods for reducing the numbers of parasites. However, they do not completely eliminate the hazard, nor do they minimize it to an acceptable level.

It should be noted that a typical home freezer does not maintain temperatures lower than 0° F (-18° C). The above USDA guidelines call for freezing and storing fish at -4°F (-20°C) or below for 7 days (total time). The answer to the problem is to increase the storing time at -4°F (-20°C) to at least 10 days.

Home refrigerator	Butcher's cooler
36° - 40 F° (2° - 4° C)	32 F ° (0° C)
Home freezer	Butcher's freezer
0° F (-18° C)	-25° F (- 32° C)

Chapter 4

Cleaning Mullet

Mullet can be prepared in many different ways. How the fish is processed depends on:
- The planned method of cooking.
- The size of the fish.

Mullet is not a huge fish, averaging about one foot in length and just over one pound in weight, but there are mullet that are 24 inches long and can weigh up to three pounds. The size of the fish determines the cleaning method that will be employed and the latter influences the cooking method.

Unless a fish is of a very large size, it is not filleted but only gutted and cleaned on the outside. The gills and all traces of blood are removed, especially the bloody kidney line along the back of the fish. Previously frozen fish can be thawed in a refrigerator or under cold running water, brined and smoked.

1. Smoking is the preferred method of processing mullet. Mullet has a strong skin and quite large scales, but it makes little sense to remove them as:
- The procedure is messy and time consuming.
- Scales protect the skin and flesh from heat. There is less danger of skin breaking apart due to excessive heat and the fish ends up nicely smoked and juicy.

Most fish to be smoked are split open (butterfly style) or left whole. In both cases the head and the entrails are removed.

2. The fish can be fried, baked or stewed. The scales must be removed as they are non-edible and unsightly. Poaching (cooking in liquid) is not recommended as mullet is a very tender, oily fish.

3. Large mullet can be filleted. If the fillet will be smoked, leave the skin on. The fish has an oily layer between the skin and its flesh and this oil makes mullet tender and juicy. Additionally, the tender meat tends to fall apart when the skin is removed which we don't want to occur in a smoker.

Dressing Mullet "Butterfly" Style

Mullet is usually split open "butterflied" or gutted and left whole. In both cases the head is cut off. If you have just a few fish, you may perform the entire operation in a sink. Scaling is messy but you can place the fish inside of a trash bag and scrape off the scales. They will fly left and right so the best idea is to do it outside. Any dull knife, spoon or proper fish scaler will do the job, just make sure that the scales are wet. Wet scales come off much easier than dry ones.

Photo 4.1 Cutting the head off.

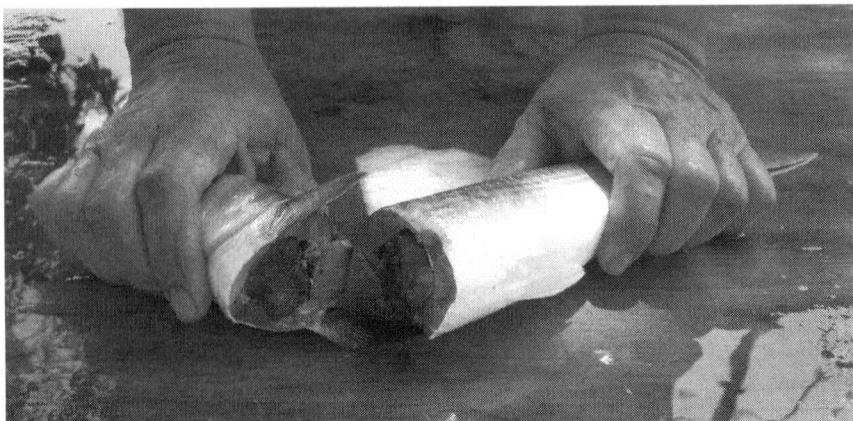

Photo 4.2 A larger mullet has a stronger back bone and sometimes the knife will not cut through it. You can easily break the fish in two.

Chapter 4 - Cleaning Mullet   37

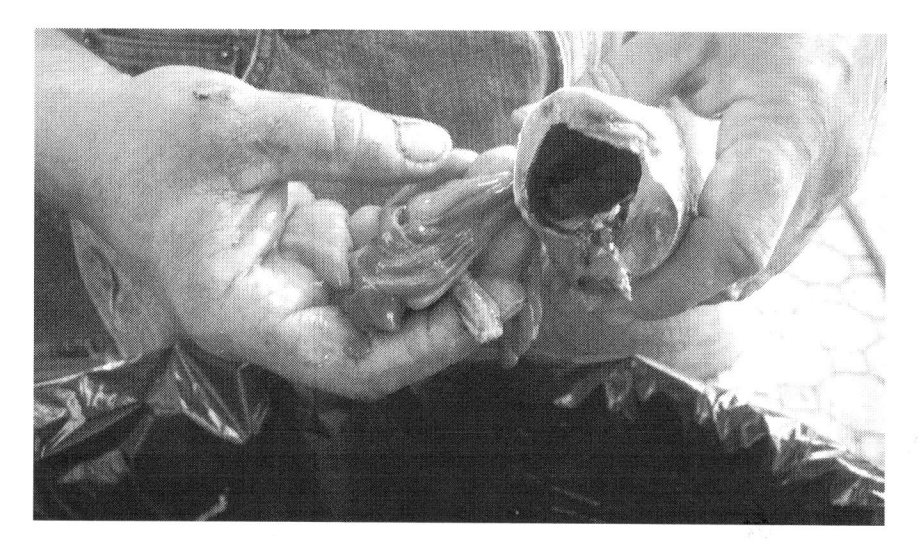

Photo 4.3 Gently squeeze the body of the fish and all entrails can be removed with your fingers. It is much easier than it looks.

You may keep edible parts such as gizzard or roe. Mullet and shad are the only fish that have gizzards. These can be fried up just like chicken gizzards. With a little hot sauce they're wonderful!

Photo 4.4 There are no entrails left, the black stomach lining can easily be brushed away.

Photo 4.5 Scrape scales with knife, scaler tool or a spoon from the tail towards the front. Scaling can be done at any time, before the fish is gutted or after. It is easier to remove scales when they are wet.

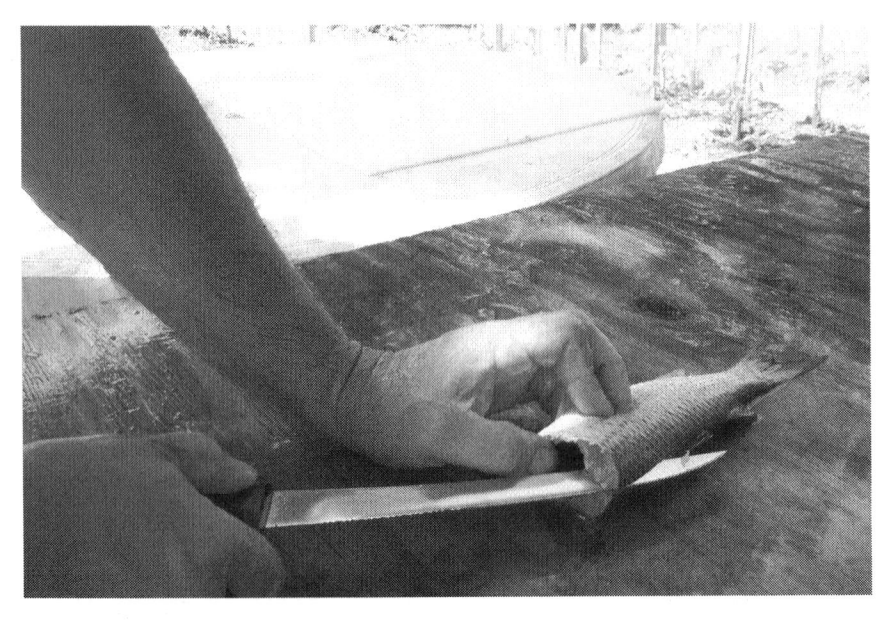

Photo 4.6 Make the incision from the back towards the belly over the back bone. Don't cut through the belly.

Chapter 4 - Cleaning Mullet 39

Photo 4.7 The back is split but the belly remains intact.

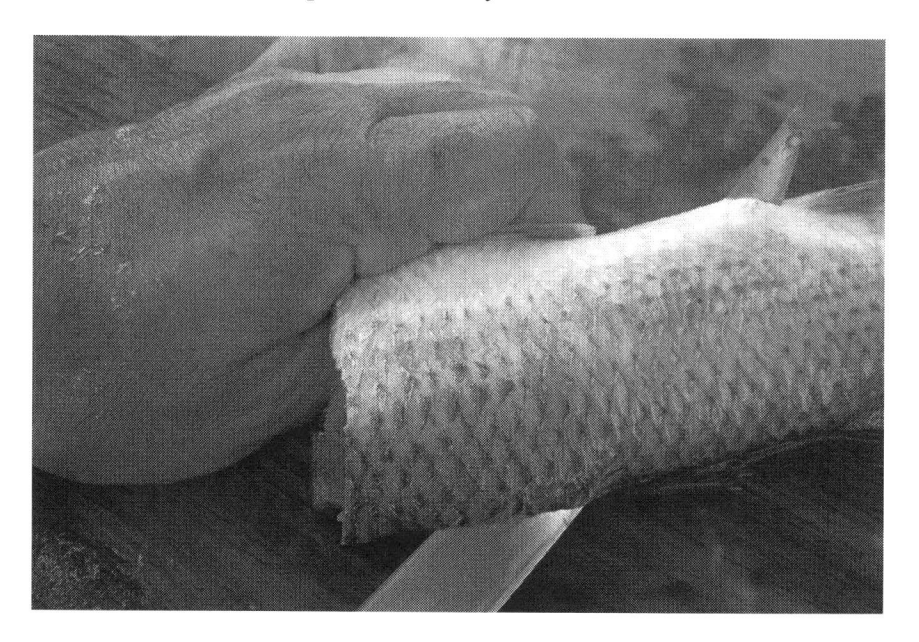

Photo 4.8 Continue cutting through the rib cage towards the vent. As mentioned previously, the belly is not cut. Come out with the knife through the vent, cutting towards the tail and cutting above the back bone.

Photo 4.9 Continue cutting to the tail.

Photo 4.10 Split mullet "butterfly" style.

Chapter 4 - Cleaning Mullet 41

Photo 4.11 The stomach lining is covered with black film which is easily brushed and hosed away.

Photo 4.12 The kidney line runs along the back bone and it must be removed. It is bitter and will promote the growth of bacteria. It can be scraped with a brush or even your finger, then rinsed away.

42 The Amazing Mullet

Photo 4.13 Clean mullet.

*The procedure for dressing **Whole Mullet** is very similar:*

Photo 4.14 Head is cut off and the entrails are removed.

Chapter 4 - Cleaning Mullet 43

Photo 4.15 The knife is inserted into the vent.

Photo 4.16 The belly is cut towards the front.

Photo 4.17 The stomach liner.

Photo 4.18 Stomach liner and the kidney line are brushed away.

Chapter 4 - Cleaning Mullet 45

Photo 4.19 The fish is rinsed.

Photo 4.20 Clean whole mullet.

Processing a Large Mullet Catch

If you catch 50 or more fish at the time, you have to properly plan your cleaning operation. A hose with running water is a must and a stiff nylon brush is needed. It will take hours before all the fish are cleaned, washed, and brined, so large containers filled with ice are needed. Get some help if you can. Keep in mind that the brined fish must dry out first before smoke is applied, then it is smoked, cooled, packed, etc. This is a whole day's affair.

Note: if the fish will be brined, don't forget to prepare the brine a day earlier and keep it in a refrigerator or freezer. Salty water (brine) freezes at a lower temperature than fresh water. Large amounts of brine kept in a freezer overnight will develop only a little ice on top. The disadvantage of preparing brine in the last moment is that it will not be cold, unless large amounts of ice are added to the water. This makes determining the strength of the brine much harder, besides it consumes valuable time that should be dedicated to processing fish. If the brine is not icy cold, the fish starts to spoil faster and although it will be fine to consume, nevertheless its shelf life will be shorter.

Photo 4.21 The author always keeps two gallons of 80° SAL brine in a freezer to be prepared for any unexpected fish catch.

Chapter 4 - Cleaning Mullet 47

Photo 4.22 A nice catch of 63 mullet, 2 sheepshead, 1 tilapia and a blue crab. The fish were caught at night with a cast net from a little bridge in St. Petersburg, Florida.

Photo 4.23 A job of this size must be well organized: water hose, ice, large covered containers, table, garbage can, brush, knives, paper towels, etc.

Photo 4.24 Freshly caught and cleaned fish are *always kept on ice* until ready for brining. There are too many fish to transfer directly from the cleaning station to the brining container as the first ones will remain in the brine too long becoming overly salty. Once cleaned, the fish will be immersed in brine.

Chapter 4 - Cleaning Mullet

Filleting

Sheepshead, also known as the "convict" fish is often caught along with mullet. The filleting procedure for both fish is the same. Sheepshead has been chosen for demonstration purpose as its body contains a thicker flesh.

Photo 4.25 Sheepshead.

Photo 4.26 A cut is made around the gill cover.

Photo 4.27 A cut is made on the top side of the fish as close to the backbone as possible.

Photo 4.28 The tail is held with the fingers and the knife separates flesh from the skin using a sawing motion. On the underside of the skin you can find a red and oily layer of flesh. This where most of the fish flavor is present. This layer develops a stronger fishy smell the longer it sits in the freezer.

A lighter-flavored fillet can be produced by deep skinning the mullet and discarding this layer of fish tissue.

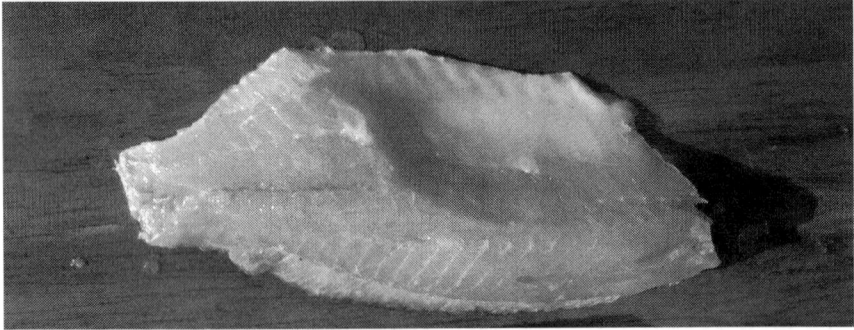

Photo 4.29 and Photo 4.30 The hardest part is to cut over the rib cage. It is difficult to feel the rib cage when a fish is small.

Photo 4.31 Filleted fish.

Chapter 4 - Cleaning Mullet

There is no need to cut off the head or gut the fish when filleting. Make sure that the knife is sharp and take your time. The disadvantage is that even a skilled operator must throw away a lot of usable meat that is located around the back bone.

An average mullet is a small fish about one foot long and weighing around one pound. You can occasionally catch bigger individuals, up to 24 inches long and weighing 2-3 pounds. Those are better suited for filleting.

Cleaning Fish Without Cutting

The entrails can be removed without cutting fish. The procedure is often used for baking stuffed fish.

Photo 4.32 The entrails will be removed through the gill opening. The fish should be scaled first.

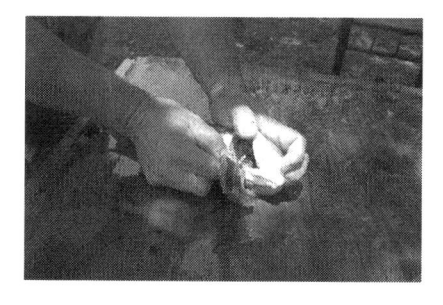

Photo 4.33 Gills can be removed with fingers. Knife or scissors may be needed on a larger fish.

Photo 4.34 Then all guts can be easily pulled out. On occasion, a mullet's stomach can present some difficulty.

Photo 4.35 A long and stiff toothbrush will scrape off the stomach lining and the red kidney line.

Photo 4.36 Fully dressed mullet which was not cut at all. Such a fish can be stuffed, baked and served elegantly on a plate.

Bleeding Fish

Bleeding fish is a phrase used to describe the removal of blood from fish. It should be performed as soon as possible when the fish are caught. Bleeding fish is performed to preserve the quality and appearance of the meat. Mullet are bled by snapping the head of the body then sticking the index finger and middle fingers in their gills and ripping them out. The blood immediately starts to squirt out for about 10 seconds. There are a few main advantages to bleeding mullet: it results in whiter meat when filleted, there is a less fishy flavor present, and the bacteria spoilage is slowed down.

Photo 4.37 Bled mullet.

Chapter 5

Fish Brine

Stronger brines require a shorter time of brining. A large fish and fat fish absorb salt slowly. Only fine non-iodized salt can be used as the iodized salt can impart a bitter flavor to the fish. The best solution is to use a brine tester or to use the brine tables provided. The fish is normally brined with a heavy brine for the following reasons:

- Its meat contains very little salt and a lot of water. These are ideal conditions for the development of meat spoiling bacteria.
- Fish is home to an unusually high concentration of bacteria.
- By placing fish in a strong 80 degrees brine we are performing an all out attack on the bacteria preventing them from growing.

A 70-80% brine can be employed for all the common types of fish. Salt penetrates the flesh of fish very rapidly and when the brine is strong (70-80 degrees), the brining times are relatively short, between 1 and 2 hours. Brines stronger than 80 degrees can deposit salt crystals on the surface of the fish skin, creating unattractive white patches that can be difficult to remove. We can get better and more uniform salt penetration if the brining times are longer but that will call for a 40 degrees solution. In an even weaker brine, for example a poultry strength brine (21 degrees), fish may be left overnight.

Fish that will be smoked should be *salted* or *brined* first. Brining provides the following advantages:

- Improves the flavor and appearance of the fish.
- Improves texture-makes flesh much stronger which is important when fish is hung.
- Prevents the growth of bacteria.

Salt penetrates fish easier in places that are open or cut than through the skin. A medium size whole mullet should remain in 80 degrees brine for about 2 hours. Fillets need to be submerged in the same brine for only 15-30 minutes.

A typical 80 degrees brine:

1 gallon water
2.25 lbs salt (4 cups)
1 lb brown sugar
2 Tbs Cure #1
1/3 cup lemon juice
1 Tbs garlic powder
1 Tbs onion powder
1 Tbs allspice powder
1 Tbs white pepper

Let's make something absolutely clear - smoked fish needs salt. This can be accomplished by sprinkling fish with salt or immersing fish in salty brine. All other ingredients may influence the flavor of smoked fish, but only a little. Those ingredients may as well be added to the fish during a meal. In addition you can serve fish with one of many classic sauces, which will influence the flavor of the fish much more than adding pepper, sugar or lime to brine. Those ingredients will work better when brining times are longer, but you have to decrease the strength of the brine, or the fish will end up too salty.

One gallon of brine is sufficient for 4 pounds of fish. Other ingredients like sugar and spices should be added to the solution after the correct brine strength has been established. Fish pieces should be completely immersed in brine and covered with a weight plate. The temperature of the brine should not exceed 60° F (15.5° C) at the start of brining. If the brining time exceeds 4 hours, the solution must be placed in a refrigerator (38° F) or ice should be added to the brine. Adding ice will change the strength of the brine and a better solution is to add re-usable ice packs. Keep in mind that brine loses its strength in time as salt penetrates the meat leaving behind a weaker solution. When brining times are long the solution's strength should be periodically checked with a brine tester and readjusted accordingly.

Chapter 5 - Brining

Making Brine

There isn't a universal brine and every book and recipe provides customized instructions. Salt of different density and weight (table salt, Morton® Kosher, Diamond® Kosher) is measured with different instruments such as spoons, cups, ounces, pounds, kilograms - water measured by cups, quarts, gallons, liters... a total mess.

The main advantage of making your own brine is that you have total control over it and there is no guessing involved. Firstly, it makes no sense at all to talk about curing time if we don't specify the strength of a brine. We can mix ½ cup salt with one quart of water or we can add 5 cups salt into one gallon of water and it is obvious that curing times will be different though both brines will do the job. To prepare your own brine in a professional way you need two things:

1. Buy a brine tester. They are so cheap that there is no excuse not to have one. The salinometer or salometer (brinometer) consists of a float with a stem attached, marked in degrees. The instrument will float at its highest level in a saturated brine, and will read 100 degrees (26.4 % salt solution). This is known as a fully saturated brine at 60° F. In weaker brines the stem will float at lower levels and the reading will be lower. With no salt present the reading will be 0. To make brine put some water one into a suitable container, add some salt, insert a brine tester and read the scale. Want a stronger solution: add more salt. Need a weaker brine: add more water, it is that simple. Keep in mind that a salinometer's scale measures the density of a solution containing salt and water. Once you add other ingredients they will alter the density of a solution effecting the salinometer reading, while the salinity of the brine will actually be the same.

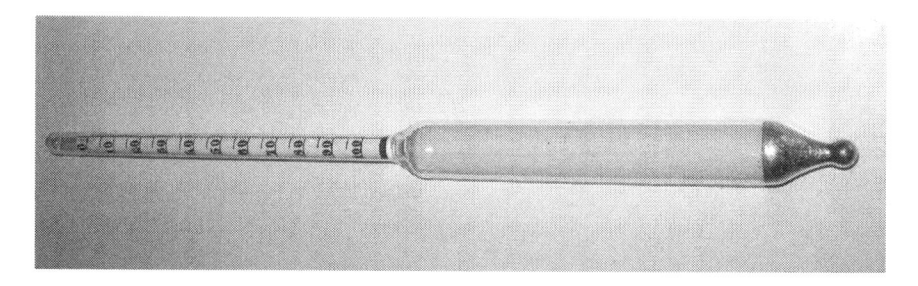

Photo 5.1 Brine tester.

Photo 5.2 Salt is added to water until the correct brine strength is obtained.

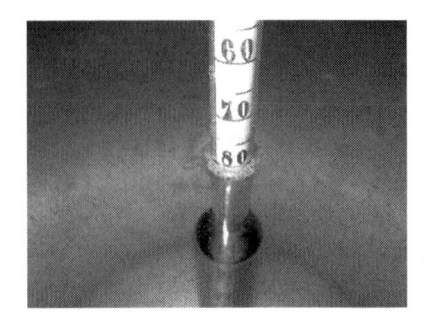

Photo 5.4 Brine tester floating in brine.

2. Learn how to use brine tables.

The advantages of using tables are many:
- you can calculate the strength of any recipe you come across.
- you can find out how much salt to add to 1 gallon of water to create a particular brine strength.
- you don't have to worry whether you use table salt, Morton® kosher salt or Diamond® kosher salt.

Brine Tables are especially useful when making a large volume of brine.

Brine at 60° F	salt (gram/liter)	salt (lb/US gallon)	% salt by weight
10°	26.4	0.22	2.64
20°	53.8	0.46	5.28
30°	79.2	0.71	7.91
40°	105.6	0.98	10.55
50°	132.0	1.26	13.19
60°	158.4	1.56	15.83
70°	184.8	1.88	18.47
80°	211.2	**2.23**	21.11
90°	237.6	2.59	23.75
100°	264.0	2.98	26.39

Chapter 5 - Brining

To make 80° brine we need to add 2.23 pounds of salt to 1 gallon of water. If you need a smaller quantity of 80° brine, add 1.1 lb salt to half-gallon of water. *The procedure is simple and fast.* The tables cover brine from 0 - 100° in one degree intervals. There are separate tables for US and UK gallons which can be obtained on the internet.

Photo 5.5 Four gallons brine that was prepared a day earlier. It is still partially frozen.

Photo 5.6 When mixing ice with water, it is advisable to re-check brine strength with a tester.

Seawater contains approximately 3.695 % of salt which corresponds to 14 degrees salometer (°SAL). At 100 degrees the brine is fully saturated and contains 26.395 % of salt. 1 US gallon of water weighs 8.33 lbs. 1 US gallon = 3.8 liters = 3.8 kilograms

Brining Times

The brining time depends on the size of the fish and the salt concentration of the brine. It is hard to derive time for fish fillets, fish with the skin on, and little fish or pieces of fish. It is logical to expect that the fish fillet will be over salted if immersed for the same time in the same brine as a large fish. When brining many types of fish of different sizes it will be a good idea to use separate containers and classify fish according to its species and size. When using a single container, place small pieces on top so they can be removed earlier. The whole fish will require a longer brining time than a fillet.

"Rule of thumb" brining times for whole fish	
Brine strength in degrees	Brining times in hours
30	10-12
50	3-4
80	1-2

Brining times for *cold smoking:*

80 degrees brine

½" fillets	-	½ hr
1" fillets	-	1 hr
1 ½" fillets	-	2 hrs

Brining times for *hot smoking:*

80 degrees brine

½" fillets	-	15 min
1" fillets	-	30 min
1 ½" fillets	-	1 hr

Influence of Salt on Fish Presentation

Fish, besides tasting good, should also look presentable and appealing. Smoked fish should have a glossy appearance, it should shine. This shine is known as "pellicle" and is due to the reaction between salt and fish proteins. Salt diffuses inside the fish and the fish proteins swell and release juices. These in turn are drawn out by the salt to the surface of the fish where they create an artificial shiny skin. Think of it as applying shoe paste to give your boots a shoe shine. Once the fish was salted or removed from the brine, it needs around two hours (or more) of resting (drying) time for pellicle to appear. Of course the unsmoked fish will have a grayish shine and the smoked fish will exhibit a golden gloss. Keep in mind that if you apply dry salt with pepper and other spices, this gloss will be less noticeable as the spices will remain on the surface.

What's Better Dry Salt or Brine

If you catch one or two fish, sprinkling with salt may be more practical. However, if you catch 50 or 60 mullet, then it becomes a little commercial venture and brining is a good solution. A correct strength brine can be made a day earlier and may be kept in the refrigerator until needed. The advantage of using brine is that once you choose the strength of the brine you like, the product you make will always be consistent and top quality. The brine strength remains constant and you simply adjust brining time according to the size of the fish. All you need is a timer and you will know after the first session whether 15 minutes was a sufficient time for your fillet. Sprinkling fish with dry mixture has very little to do with science, but is an acceptable method for curing fish at home. There is no salt wasted when sprinkling fish with dry mix.

Many small producers use dry mix only for reasons of economics as less space and equipment is required. The processing time is also shorter as fish does not need to be dried before the smoke is applied. On the other hand, brined fish is wet and needs to drain and dry out before the smoke can be applied. In addition much salt will be wasted when brine is discarded. Commercial producers test brine for microbiological spoilage and can reuse it again. A hobbyist should use brine only once.

There are many ready to apply dry mixes that can be used for general cooking or smoking fish. Creole Seasoning is an excellent dry mix for smoking mullet made by Zatarain's, New Orleans, LA.

More About Salt

For brining purposes both table salt and kosher salt will work equally well in terms of providing the desired effects, though kosher salt, particularly Diamond® Crystal kosher salt dissolves more readily. What is important to remember is that kosher salts are less dense than ordinary table salts and measure quite differently from a volume standpoint. Kosher salt has larger crystals and is bulkier. For example a given weight of Diamond® Crystal takes up nearly twice the volume as the same weight of table salt.

The list below shows approximate equivalent amounts of different salts:

Table Salt	1 cup	292 g (10.3 oz)
Morton® Kosher Salt	1-1/3 to 1-1/2 cups	218 g (7.7 oz)
Diamond® Crystal Kosher Salt	2 cups	142 g (5 oz)

As you can see it is always advisable to weigh out your salt.

Brining and smoking fish is a lot of trial and error and record keeping. Notes should be made for future reference.

Chapter 6

Smoking Fish

Fish has always played a very important part in our diet being a precious commodity, especially in areas without direct access to water. For those reasons preservation played a major role and taste was less important. Preservation was achieved by storing heavily salted fish in barrels where they were kept for months at a time. Caravans were able to move salted fish large distances and all the consumer had to do was to soak the fish in water to remove excess salt. Another technique relied on air drying to remove moisture from the meat thus eliminating favorable conditions for the growth of bacteria. Smoking fish was also effective as it prevented some bacteria from growing and removed moisture at the same time.

Heavy salting of the fish is practiced today in mostly undeveloped nations and everywhere else we strive to give fish the best taste and flavor. And there is no doubt whatsoever that smoked fish tastes the best. Fish like other meats can be smoked by different smoking methods. The texture and flavor of the fish will depend on smoke temperature, the length of smoking, and to a lesser degree on the type of wood used for smoking.

Smoking - Reasons

Man discovered that smoking was a very effective tool in preserving fish. Besides enhancing the taste and look, it also increases the fish's longevity. It helps preserve the meat by slowing down the spoilage of fat and growth of bacteria. Smoking fish leads to more water loss, and results in a saltier and drier product, which naturally increases its shelf life. The advantages of smoking fish are numerous:

- Slows down the growth of bacteria.
- Prevents fats from developing a rancid taste.
- Extends the shelf life of the product.
- Develops a new taste and flavor.
- Changes the color, smoked products shine and look better.

The main reason to smoke fish at home today is to produce a product that cannot be obtained in a typical store. One can order traditionally made products on the Internet but they will be very expensive.

What is Smoking ?

Smoking meat is exactly what the name implies: flavoring meat with smoke. Using any kind of improvised device will do the job as long as the smokehouse is made from environmentally safe material. As long as smoke contacts the meat surface it will impart its flavor to the meat. The strength of the flavor depends mainly on the time and density of the smoke.

Smoke is a mixture of air and gases created during wood combustion. What we see is a stream of gases such as nitrogen, carbon dioxide, carbon monoxide, water vapor, and sulphur dioxide that carry unburned particles such as tar, resins, soot and air borne ash. The actual composition of the smoke depends on the type of wood, its moisture content, combustion temperature, and the amount of available air. It is estimated that smoke consists of about 10,000 individual components and a few hundred of these are responsible for the development of a smoky flavor. The air draft, which might be considered the smokehouse sucking power, sucks in the outside air and combustion gases that in turn attract solid unburned particles such as soot, ash and others. This stream rushes inside of the smoking chamber where it collides with hanging meats and with the walls of the chamber. A stronger air draft and higher temperature increase the energy of the smoke which results in more intense smoking.

This explains why the cold smoking process is much slower than the hot smoking method. The amount of moisture on the surface of a product plays a role in color formation and the color develops faster when the surface is wetter. This also results in a much darker color as particles such as tar and soot easily stick to the surface. That creates a barrier to smoke penetration and as a rule the surface of the product receiving smoke should be dry or at least feel tacky to the touch.

Smoking may or may not be followed by cooking. Some products are only smoked at low temperatures and are never cooked. These products are still safe to eat. Lox has a long shelf life and yet this fish product is not cooked. Generally we may say that smoking fish in most cases consists of two steps:
- Smoking
- Cooking

After smoking is done we increase the temperature to about 170° F (76° C) to start cooking. The smoked fish must be cooked to 145° F (63° C) internal temperature and here the quality and insulation of the smoker plays an important role. Nevertheless, the main smoking process is performed below 160° F (71° C). Smoked fish are usually eaten cold at a later date. Many great recipes require that smoked products hang for a designated time to lose more weight and become drier. It is only then that they are ready for consumption. Fish like other meats can be smoked by different smoking methods and the taste and shelf life will depend on smoke temperature and the length of smoking.

Cold smoking – fish is smoked below 80° F (26° C) from 1-5 days. Temperatures above 80° F (26° C) will cook the fish. If the temperature of the fish flesh exceeds 84° F (29° C) for longer than a few minutes the protein will be coagulated and parts of the fish will be cooked. Such fish will not have the elasticity and texture of the properly cold smoked product. Cold smoked fish is still considered raw meat as it was never exposed to high temperatures. That is why it has to be heavily salted or brined at 16% salt (about 65 degrees brine) or higher to provide safety for the consumer.

The longer the smoking period the more moisture is removed, the drier the product becomes, and of course it develops a longer shelf life. Its color also changes from gold to brown. This method of smoking can last up to a few weeks and the fish will have excellent keeping qualities. It should be noted that the final product will taste much saltier and its texture will be much harder. After prolonged cold smoking the fish has lost enough moisture not to be cooked at all. A typical fish prepared that way is salmon or sturgeon. Cold smoking requires heavy brine and longer brining times. Fish that were cold smoked hold well together and can be very finely sliced which cannot be done if the fish were hot smoked. Cold smoking is not a continuous process, it is stopped (no smoke) a few times to allow fresh air into the smoker. In XVIII century brick built smokehouses a fire was started every morning. It smoldered as long as it could and if it stopped, it would be restarted again the following morning. Because of the time and costs involved this method is rarely used today.

Hot smoking – fish are smoked and cooked at the same time. Hot smoking requires a lighter brine and a smokehouse temperature above 90° F (32° C). The fish are smoked/cooked from one to five hours. The fish can be smoked/baked in 30 minutes when the applied temperature is 300-350° F (150-180° C). Hot smoking is a commonly used method today.

The shelf life of the hot smoked product is shorter than its cold smoked counter part and the product must be kept under refrigeration. Hot smoking is basically performed in three stages:

1. A preliminary smoking/drying period at 86° F (30° C) during which the skin is hardened to prevent breakage. The air dampers are fully open for maximum air flow and moisture removal. This period lasts from 30-60 minutes.

2. A heavy smoke is applied for about 30-45 minutes with the exit smoke damper left at ¼ open position. The temperature is gradually raised to 122° F (50° C).

3. The temperature is raised to 176° F (80° C) and the fish is cooked to 145° F (63° C) internal temperature for a minimum of 30 minutes. Depending on the size of the fish this stage may last from 30–60 minutes. A light smoke may be maintained. When the temperature is raised to 176-194° F (80-90°C) we are smoking/cooking the fish until its meat flakes out easily when pressed with a knife or a fork. The cooking process will be shorter but the fish will taste drier. Fish is considered done when cooked to 145° F internal temperature. Typical fish fillets smoking times are 2-5 hours depending on the size. When smoking is finished, the fish should be cooled rapidly to the ambient (50° F, 10° C) and then to lower temperatures (38° F, 3° C) to prevent the growth of microorganisms. This cooling process should be accomplished within 12 hours.

In an open fire smokehouse, the rear of the chamber is receiving most of the heat and re-arranging smoke sticks is a welcome idea. If the fish feels moist, it is a sign that there is too much wet smoke inside and the draft must be open more. The back of the fish or the skin of the fillet should face the back of the smoker. This allows for better judgment of the fish color and protects the flesh from higher temperatures that are normally found in the back of the smoker. When using a few levels of smoke sticks place the upper row first, then after 5-10 minutes the lower one, then the lowest one. If all three levels were placed in a smokehouse at the same time, the upper most row will get the least of the available heat during drying. On the other hand it will get the most moisture which will gather from the smokesticks below.

Smoke Generation

Smoke can be generated by:

- Burning firewood. Due to the danger of flames this method is limited to smokers with a separate fire pit.

Chapter 6 - Smoking Mullet

- Heating wood chips or sawdust with an electrical wire (barbecue starter). Once started they will keep on smoldering and the wire starter is not needed anymore.
- Heating wood chips or sawdust over a gas flame or placing wood chips over hot coals. This method is commonly used when barbecuing meats.

The preferred method to handle wood chips or sawdust is to place them in a stainless steel pan, about 10-12" in diameter, not higher than 4", otherwise smoke may be too hot. To sustain smoke production more wood chips must be added. The wood chips should be kept together in a conical pile so that they will smolder and not burn. The moment they spread, they make contact with more air and are more inclined to burn. The same applies when adding wood chips directly on hot coals or ashes, keep them in a pile and if the flames start to grow bigger, add more wood chips to cut off the supply of fresh air. After a while a natural rhythm of adding sawdust will be established and the whole process will go on smoothly.

Photo 6.1 Hot plate.

Photo 6.2 Barbecue starter.

If smoking stops, the barbecue starter or hot plate is reconnected again. If the sawdust bursts into flames, any common spray bottle can bring it under control. All small and medium size factory made smokers use these methods to generate smoke. The bigger factory made models employ a free standing smoke generation unit that is connected with the smoker by a short pipe. Draft control plays no role here since an electrical blower blows the smoke into the smoker. Industrial smokehouses choose different methods of smoke generation but that does not necessarily mean that the quality is better. One method involves pressing blocks of pressed sawdust against rotating wheels. The resistance creates high temperatures and the block of wood starts to smoke. It's like cutting a piece of wood with a dull saw blade; it starts to smoke because of the heat generated.

Photo 6.3 Drum smoker.

Burning whole logs is not easy and requires continuous attention. It is much easier to insert an electrical heating element at the bottom of the smoker.

Wood for Smoking

Any hardwood is fine, but evergreen trees like fir, spruce, pine, or others cause problems. They contain too much resin and the finished product has a turpentine flavor to it. It also develops a black color due to the extra soot from the smoke, which in turn makes the smoker dirtier too. And of course you cannot use any wood that was previously pressure treated, painted, or commercially manufactured. The type of wood used is responsible for the final color of the smoked product and it can also influence its taste but only to a small degree. All fruit and citrus trees have a light to medium sweet flavor and are excellent for poultry and ham. Many say that cherry wood is the best. Oak, available all over the world, is probably the most commonly used wood for smoking. It has always been very popular in England. It produces a brown color. If hickory is used, the color will have a more vivid red tint in it. Hickory is popular in Southern regions of the U.S., but is little known outside the country. Alder was traditionally used for smoking salmon in the Pacific Northwest. Wood types can be mixed to create custom flavors. For instance, walnut, which has a heavy smoke flavor, can be mixed with apple wood to create a milder version. For practical reasons a home sausage maker will probably use oak or hickory most of the time.

Fish Flesh Color

Meat color is determined largely by the amount of myoglobin (protein) a particular animal carries. The more myoglobin the darker the meat. To some extent oxygen use can be related to the animal's general level of activity: muscles that are used frequently such as a chicken's legs need more oxygen. As a result, they develop a darker color unlike a chicken's breast which is white due to little exercise.

Fish float in water and need less muscle energy to support their skeletons. Most fish meat is white, with some red meat around the fins, tail, and the more active parts of the fish which are used for swimming. Most fish don't have myoglobin at all. There are some Antarctic cold water fish that have myoglobin but it is confined to the hearts only (flesh of the fish remains white but the heart is a rosy color. The red color of some fish, such as salmon and trout, is due to astaxanthin, a naturally occurring pigment in the crustaceans they eat. Most salmon we buy is farm raised and is fed a prepared commercial diet that even includes antibiotics, its meat is anything but pink. The only reason that farmed raised salmon flesh is pink is that canthaxanthin (colorant) is added to the food the fish eats.

The pink color of the smoked meat is due to the nitrite reaction with myoglobin. As most of the fish don't have myoglobin the meat is not going to be pink and that explains why very few fish recipes include cure. In addition, nitrites are not allowed in all species of fish used for smoking. The Food and Drug Administration currently allows nitrites to be used in salmon, sablefish, shad, chubs, and tuna. Why out of the millions of species of fish swimming in the ocean, only five species can be cured with nitrite? What made those fish so special was a question that puzzled me for a long time. After much research and no progress, a letter of inquiry was sent to the Food Safety and Inspection Service. And here was the answer to my inquiry:

"The reason nitrite is approved for use in those species is because someone submitted a petition for its use in those specific fish. Other species can be added through additional petitions."

Smoking Mullet

All fish may be smoked but the fatty ones absorb smoke better, stay moister during smoking and taste better. Fat content of different fish:

Lean fish	< 2.5%
Medium fat fish	2.5 – 6.5%
Fat fish	> 6.5%

The same species of fish, depending where they live (Europe, Atlantic or Pacific Ocean), may have a significantly different fat content in their flesh. Some of the lean fish: cod, flounder, grouper, haddock, hake, halibut, perch, pike, pollock, porgies, rockfish, snake eels, snapper, soles, tuna, whiting. Some of the fat fish: bluefish, carp, freshwater eels, herring, mackerel, mullet, sablefish, salmon, shad, trout, and whitefish.

The process of smoking mullet consists of the following stages:
- Cleaning-covered in Chapter 4
- Brining-covered in Chapter 5
- Drying.
- Smoking.
- Cooking
- Cooling.
- Storing.

Chapter 6 - Smoking Mullet

After the fish is cleaned it is submitted to a brief period of curing:
- Sprinkling fish with salt and spices *or*
- Immersing fish in brine

Photo 6.4 Mullet in brine.

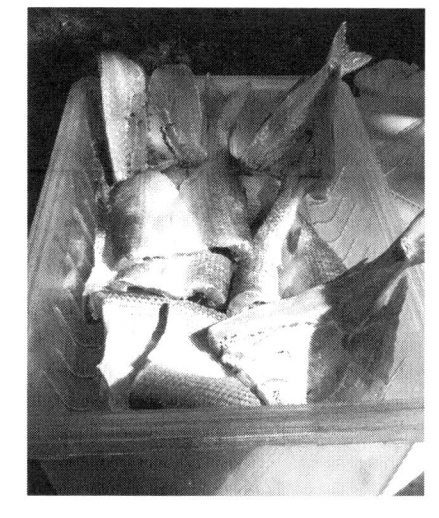

Photo 6.5 Mullet is drained, then patted dry with paper towels.

Hanging/Drying Fish

A fish that was properly dried will acquire color much faster than a wet one and will also develop a better taste. After brining the fish are carefully rinsed under cold running water to remove salt crystals and any traces of spices. The fish are then placed in a draughty area (fan works well) until they feel dry or at least tacky to touch. It is a good idea to place small fish pieces on smoking screens from the very beginning of the drying process. Brush screens lightly with oil so the fish will not stick to them.

The characteristic flavor of the fish is mainly due to salt and smoke but the texture of its flesh is greatly influenced by drying. A fish that was properly dried will acquire color much faster and will also develop a better taste. Weaker brines or not salting fish at all leaves smoked fish with a rather dull appearance. The longer hanging time, the better the results. A 1 hour period may be considered minimum. For a large fish a 12 hour drying time is not unusual.

Fish can be dried inside of a smokehouse, but the smoke must not be generated yet. The smoke exit damper should be fully open to allow for the removal of moisture.

Photo 6.6 Mullet is placed on screens and submitted to additional drying. If the weather is warm, the fish should be dried in a smokehouse.

Pellicle

Salted fish, when allowed to dry, develop a type of shiny secondary skin known as "pellicle". This gloss is due to the swelling of the protein caused by the salt in brine. Proteins dissolve in brine and create a sticky exudate on the surface. The longer the brined fish are permitted to hang, the better the gloss they develop. The best gloss develops with 70-80% brine. Pellicle helps in smoking and the final product has a nice glossy color. That normally requires 2-3 hours and is sufficient time to dry the fish for smoking.

Chapter 6 - Smoking Mullet

Photo 6.7 Mullet are drying, at about 110-120° F (43-49° C), until they feel dry or at least tacky to touch. No smoke is applied yet.

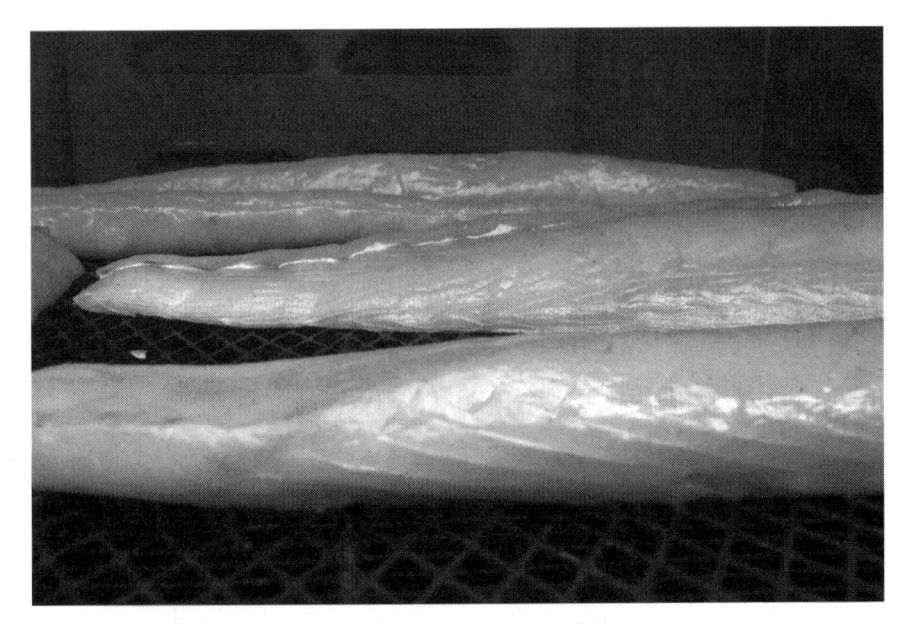

Photo 6.8 Well developed pellicle in unsmoked fish.

Photo 6.9 Beautiful golden shine in smoked fish.

The flesh of fish is delicate by nature and they have to be handled gently when hanging them on smokesticks or hooks. There are a few commonly

Chapter 6 - Smoking Mullet

used methods of securing fish for smoking such as:
- Placing fillets or smaller pieces of fish on a screen, making sure they don't touch each other. Place small fish pieces on smoking screens right from the beginning of the drying process. Brush screens lightly with oil to prevent sticking of the fish.
- Inserting sharp pointed sticks through fish gills.
- Inserting "S" shaped hooks through the gills of the fish.
- Nailing fish directly to smoke sticks.

In most cases mullet is dressed in the butterfly style and is placed on screens. The skin and the scales are left on. Whole gutted and cleaned mullet can be hung from smokesticks. The skin and the scales are left on.

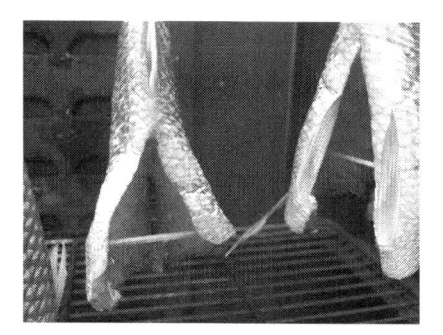

Photo 6.10 The belly should be spread open with a wooden toothpick to facilitate the flow of smoke.

Smoking

When the surface of the fish is dry, or at least feels tacky to the touch, smoke can be applied. The smoke exit damper control is maintained about 1/4 open. If the fish becomes wet again, this means that the moisture is not removed fast enough and the damper control should be opened wider. How long to smoke is an open question. Well, there isn't one universal time, use your own judgement and keep records. The size of the fish will be a deciding factor, but you can estimate smoking time by checking the color of the smoked fish as well. Mullet is a small fish so 2-3 hours of hot smoking is plenty. It is safer to smoke for two hours and check the results. Over smoked fish will acquire a bitter smoked flavor that will not go away, so it is better to be on the safe side.

As mullet is most abundant in the Gulf of Mexico and the Caribbean sea, we may assume that this is where the most fish will be smoked. The climate is hot there so the hot smoking method will be applied, although one can cold smoke fish at night hours in December, January and February. Keep in mind that *more* salt must be applied to cold smoked fish.

Photo 6.11 Mullet are smoked for 2-3 hours.

Chapter 6 - Smoking Mullet

Photo 6.12 Smoked mullet.

Photo 6.13 Packing smoked mullet into sealable plastic bags.

Cooking Temperature

The Food Safety and Inspection Service of the United States Department of Agriculture recommends cooking fish to 145° F (63° C) internal temperature. A reliable test is to insert a fork or knife into the thickest part of the fish and twist. The flesh should flake.

Cooling

Smoked meats and sausages are usually showered with cold water to let them pass through the danger zone (140-60° F, 60-16° C) as fast as possible. Afterwards they can be refrigerated. The fish smoking process ends right inside the danger zone, so in order to preserve its useful life, the fish must be cooled quickly too. Showering fish with water is not practical as much water will be trapped by the body of the fish. A better idea is to place fish in a drafty area or to use a ventilating fan to speed up cooling. Then the fish should be bagged and refrigerated or frozen.

Storing

Fish can be eaten immediately after smoking though most people will say that it tastes better when cold. Fish should be wrapped up in wax paper or foil and placed in a refrigerator where it can remain for up to 10 days. To hold it longer we have to freeze it.

Smokers

The variety of smokers are amazing and each owner swears by his own as doing the best job. Fish smokes and cooks much faster than meat or sausages so the technical expectations from a smoker are a bit lower. *A smokehouse is just a tool but smoking is time, temperature, and humidity, and how you control those parameters.* The tool does not make a quality product - YOU DO! *If you understand the smoking process you will create a top quality product in any smoker and in any conditions.* Any enclosure that will hold smoke and heat can be considered a smoker and will do a good job. To illustrate our point look at the original smoker on the next page (Photo 6.14). The design of the Concrete Block Smoker comes from the book "Meat Smoking and Smokehouse Design" by Stanley and Adam Marianski.

Chapter 6 - Smoking Mullet 77

Photo 6.14 Most unusual but effective smoker made from the stump of an old oak tree. This original set up has been in operation for 20 years. Smoker located on Poliwoda Fishing Grounds, Opole, Poland. Smoked trout ends up on a dinner plate in a popular tourist restaurant which is located on the same grounds.

Concrete Block Smoker

An excellent smoker can be built in no time by using standard 8" x 8" x 16" concrete blocks.

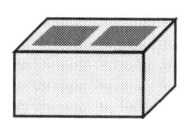

Fig. 6.1 Concrete block.

A firm support base can be made from square patio stones (12", 16", or 18") or larger prefabricated concrete slabs (30" x 30") that are used to support outside air-conditioning heat pumps. This may make an installation look prettier but is not necessary, a bare ground is fine. Just grade it well so it is leveled. A separate fire pit built from blocks is attached to the smokehouse. This way the entire smoking chamber can be utilized for smoking meats and the process is easy to control. The construction does not call for using mortar, just arranging blocks in the manner that will be most practical. Nothing stops you from using mortar to make it a permanent structure, but a strong suggestion will be to try it out a few times. Make some observations that may help you with any future decisions regarding building a permanent smoker. This is a totally flexible design and imagine that you are building a smoker like a child who is erecting a house using little building blocks. This is how this smoker is built and the only difference is that the blocks are bigger.

There are two ways of constructing a smoke delivery channel:

- Installing metal lintel over the smoke entrance opening to support the bricks above.
- Turning a block on its side creating a double opening for the smoke to flow through. This is a much simpler design.

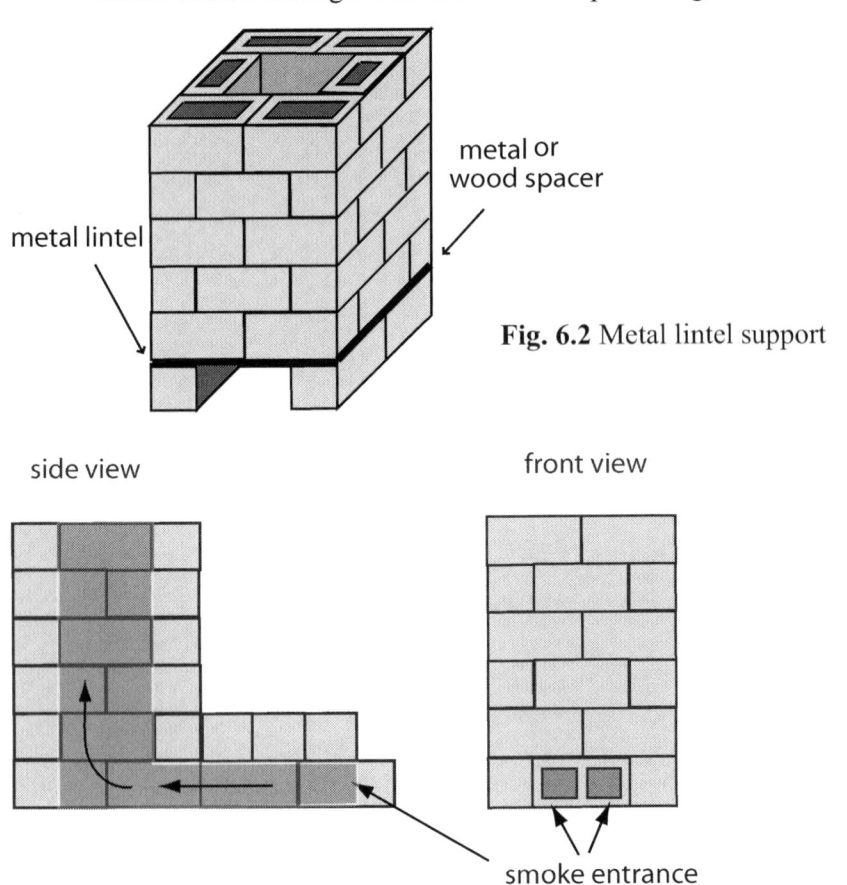

Fig. 6.2 Metal lintel support

side view

front view

Fig. 6.3 Using block for support.

Chapter 6 - Smoking Mullet

The easiest and fastest way to support the smokesticks is to place them directly on top of the smoker. A cardboard or a wooden cover rests on smokesticks. This creates ample space for the smoke to exit from the smoker. An old potatoe burlap sack has been used for that purpose for hundreds of years. Of course a flattened piece of cardboard or a piece of plywood can be used as well.

Fig. 6.4 Smokesticks on top of the smoker.

Fig. 6.5 The blocks can be spaced so that every other row can have two blocks projecting inward from the wall on each side of the smoker. This arrangement creates support for the smokesticks, screens or racks.

Neither masonry bricks, mortar, half blocks or any tools are needed. As the fire pit is on the same plane as the smoker, in order to achieve enough draft, the smoker is built of six floors and is 48" high which makes it a comfortable height to work with.

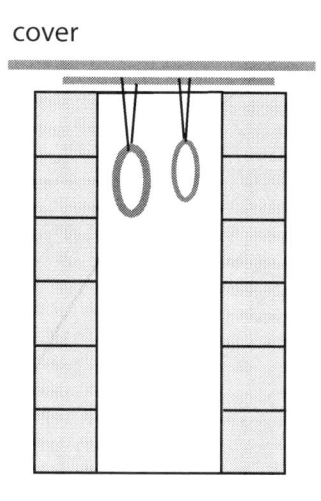

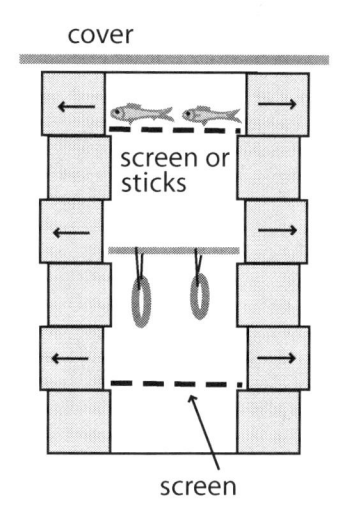

The fire pit is freely attached to the front wall. Any little smoke coming from the connection is negligible as long as there is smoke coming out of the chamber. A wet towel can be placed over the connection where the fire pit and smoker come together. A fire pit may be attached to the smoker with a mortar. As the concrete block is not designed to withhold high temperatures it is to be expected that once in a while one of the fire pit concrete blocks might crack. Obviously, the most practical solution is to replace it with a different one and go on happily smoking like before. In a six floor configuration a total of 35 blocks are used for the smoker and 7 blocks for the fire pit.

Top view at smoker and firepit

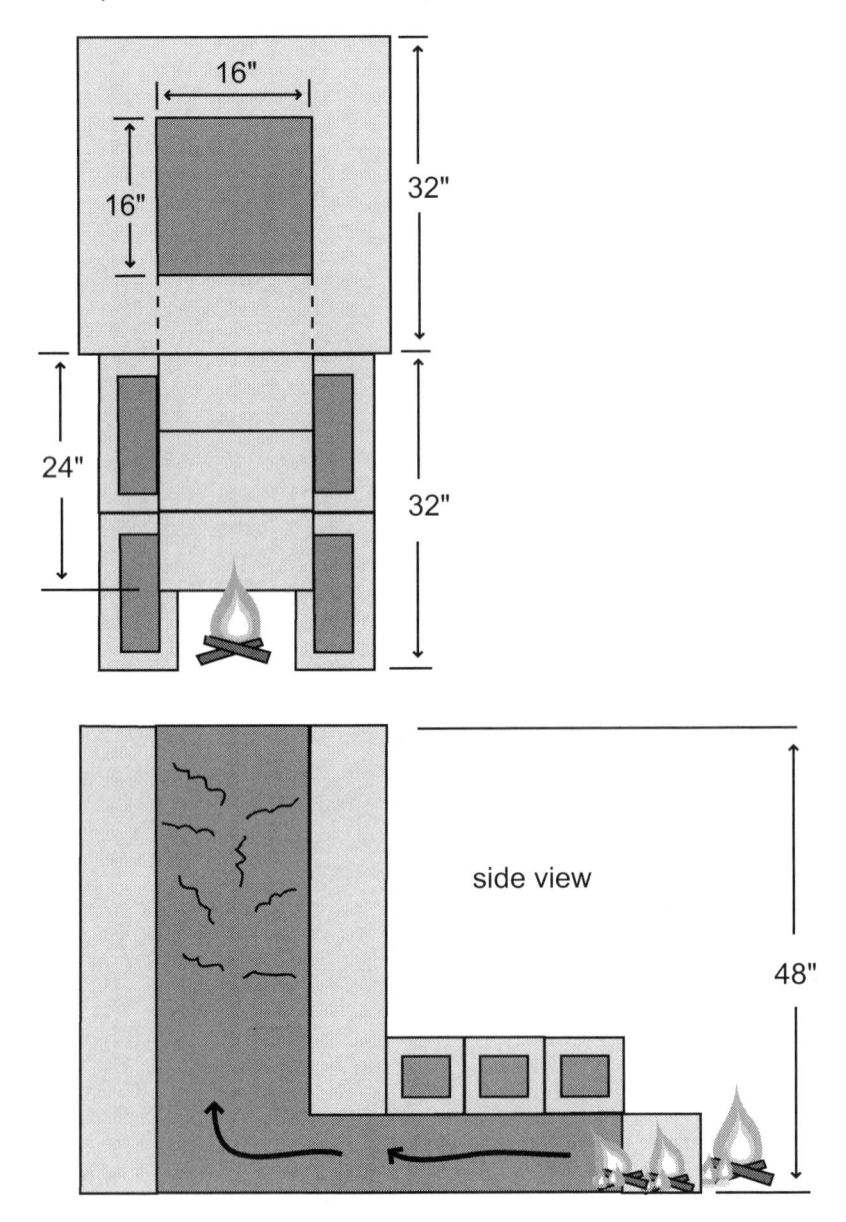

Fig. 6.6 Smoker with attached fire pit.

Chapter 7

Cooking Mullet

Mullet is a Healthy Food

In many fatty animals the flavor is concentrated in their fat, for example the texture and the color of pork fat depends greatly on a pig's diet. The tenderness of the meat is related to the "marbling" which is the amount of intramuscular fat, a key characteristic in choosing good steaks. The quality of mullet can vary depending on the environment from which the fish is taken, as this influences its feeding habits. For example, mullet that populate the Gulf Coast of Florida, which is characterized by sandy bottoms and clear waters, are considered to be of excellent quality. On the other hand, mullet taken from the Gulf Coast of Texas, which has muddy bottoms and turbid waters, are reported to display stronger oily, muddy and fishy flavors.

Mullet is not only great for smoking but can be prepared by any standard cooking method such as boiling, frying or baking. A great way to prepare smoked mullet is to make a spread or a fine pâté. Fried mullet should be cooked as quickly as possible in order not to absorb any additional fat. The fish is done when it flakes easily and its flesh is opaque. For best results, use only fresh fish. Freshly caught mullet have very bright eyes, which become opaque in time.

It would be a very monotonous staple to eat smoked mullet all the time so we have to find different methods of preparing the fish. Fish which contain a larger proportion of fat have very tender flesh and are better when smoked, fried or grilled, than poached in water. For best results in preparing a fresh fish, it is always desirable to know whether it is fat or lean. Fat fish are suitable for baking, and may also be broiled, while lean fish are best adapted to steaming, boiling and frying. Medium-fat fish are prepared like the lean, or may be dressed with strips of salt pork or bacon, and baked. Mullet are considered an oily fish, but many fish are fatter than mullet such as salmon, mackerel, shad, herring, carp, catfish, bluefish, bass, swordfish or even shark. According to their average fat content, fish are classified as:

- Very low fat - less than 2.5% fat (cod, grouper, haddock, halibut, red snapper, yellowfin tuna)
- Low fat - 2.5 - 5% fat, (**mullet**, bass, bluefish, catfish, rainbow trout, pink salmon, swordfish)
- Moderate fat - 5 - 10% fat, (herring, Spanish mackerel, Atlantic salmon, whitefish, bluefin tuna)
- High fat - more than 10% fat, (king salmon, Atlantic mackerel)

Mullet are classified as a low fat fish that contains between 2.5 and 5% fat and 20-35% of total calories come from fat. Thus it is safe to state that the mullet is a very healthy fish, as one fillet (4 oz serving) contains only 5 grams of fat and provides 134 calories. For comparison, one quarter pound (4 oz) hamburger contains 19 g of fat and provides 410 calories. Mullet are also a healthy *heart* food as they contain Omega-3 oil, which has been proven to act beneficially against heart attacks and cardiovascular diseases.

Photo 7.1 Roger Edwards with a large mullet.

Chapter 7 - Cooking Mullet

Mullet is a fatty fish and tastes great when broiled, baked or deep fried. This is done on high heat and the fish should be battered first, either in bread crumbs, flour, or in any commercially prepared batter like a beer batter seafood mix. A combination of batter and high heat creates a tasty skin on the outside and seals the juices in creating a wonderful succulent product. When deep frying, remember to remove the wire holding basket and immerse the fish directly in the hot oil (375° F), otherwise the fillets or pieces of fish will clump together and the product will resemble a loaf of bread. It will be fried on the outside with raw areas in between.

There is a great variety of home deep fryers and it is advisable to pick up a rectangular shaped one as it accommodates larger fish. Whole small mullet can be easily deep fried, pan fried or baked in an oven. Mullet does not need basting as it contains enough natural fish oil to stay moist and juicy. A large mullet can be filleted, then the fillets can be battered and fried. One can of course fillet any size fish, but a lot of meat will go to waste. The way the fish will be cleaned dictates on how the fish will be cooked. The United States Department of Agriculture recommends cooking fish to 145° F (63° C) internal temperature. Smoked fish should not be scaled, but poached, fried or baked fish must have the scales removed. All fish must be gutted and the gills must always be removed. Removing or leaving the heads on is entirely up to you. A large mullet may be stuffed:

- Leaving the head on but removing entrails through the gill opening. The fish can then be stuffed through the gill opening.
- Leaving the head on but slicing the belly open to remove entrails. The fish is stuffed, then the belly is stitched together.

Recipes

Baked Small Mullet

1. Cut off the fins and open down the belly, wash and drain.
2. Dip each fish into salted milk (or brush the fish with beaten egg), then into finely sifted bread crumbs.
3. Arrange in a row on oiled baking pan, sprinkle with a little oil or melted fat and bake in a very hot oven (450° F) ten minutes.
4. Lift out on hot platter, garnish with parsley and pieces of lemon.
5. Serve with a sauce.

Baked Large Mullet

1. Cut off the head, tail and fins. Open down the belly, wash and drain. Cut down on either side of the backbone just to the skin and pull it out, or it may be cut down just one side of the backbone so as to open it out flat in the pan (butterfly style), without removing the backbone.
2. Sprinkle fish with salt and pepper, brush with beaten egg, then blanket it with finely sifted bread crumbs to keep in all the juices. Colorlessly fried onions may be placed over it, if liked. Place in an oiled baking pan and sprinkle it with oil or melted fat.
3. Bake in hot oven (450° F) fifteen to thirty minutes, according to the thickness of the fish. The oven should be hot enough to prevent any juice from running out of the fish. It needs no basting and will be found rich in its own juices when cooked.
4. Remove whole, without breaking, to a hot platter. Garnish in any preferred way.
5. Serve with a sauce.

Baked Garam Masala Mullet Fillets

1 lb mullet fillets
1 tsp smashed garlic
1 tsp garam masala*
1 tsp chili powder
1 tsp turmeric
1 Tbsp fresh cilantro, chopped
1 Tbsp lemon juice
¼ tsp salt
1 Tbsp vegetable oil
flour, as needed
½ cup oil, for shallow frying

1. In a bowl, mix all ingredients together.
2. Dip fillets in this marinade and let it stand for 30 minutes.
3. Coat evenly with flour.
4. Fry fillets on each side in hot oil, until golden brown.

Note: * commercially made and available in Indian ethnic stores. What differentiates garam masala from curry powder is that it contains aromatic spices like cinnamon and cloves.

Fried Small Mullets or Fillets of Mullet

2 pounds mullet
Juice 1 lemon
4 tablespoons butter
1 tablespoon minced parsley
Flour
Oil
Salt

1. Roll prepared fish in salted flour.
2. Heat some oil in frying pan and fry fish until it develops a nice brown color on each side. Remove to a hot platter.
3. Melt the butter, add the lemon juice and parsley. Allow to boil up, pour over the fillets or small fish, and serve at once.

Fried Mullet Chinese Style

1 lb mullet
4 scallions, finely chopped
½ piece fresh ginger (1 inch long), finely chopped
1 Tbsp soy sauce
2 Tbsp sherry wine
½ cup water
salt and pepper to taste
½ cup peanut oil, for shallow frying
cornstarch, as needed

1. Wet the fish with soy sauce on both sides and fry in hot oil, 3 minutes each side.
2. Add the chopped ginger, scallions, sherry wine, water, salt and pepper to the fish. Cover and simmer for 15 minutes.
3. Place fish on a hot plate and pour the sauce over it. If the sauce is too thin, mix some cornstarch with cold water (1:3) and stir it in, until the sauce thickens.

Fried Mullet Fillets

2 lbs mullet fillets
Cornmeal, 1 cup
Salt and pepper

1. Season the cornmeal with salt and butter.
2. Roll fillets in the cornmeal.
3. Heat some oil in frying pan and fry fish until develops a nice brown color on each side. Remove to a hot platter.
4. Serve with Horseradish Butter or any sauce of your choice.

Fried Mullet Curry

1 lb mullet
1 Tbsp red curry paste**
2 cups coconut milk
2 Tbsp coconut palm sugar *or* brown sugar
1 Tbsp fish sauce*
3 cups vegetable oil, for deep frying

1. With a knife, score both sides of the fish in a criss-cross design.
2. Fry fish in hot oil until golden brown.
3. Heat 1 cup of coconut milk, add the curry paste and stir until smooth. Add the rest of coconut milk, bring to a boil, then add the fish.
4. Cook the fish for 2 minutes. Place the fish on a hot plate.
5. Season the sauce with sugar and fish sauce*. Pour the sauce over the fish.

Note: * commercially made and available in a supermarket.
** available in Indian ethnic grocery stores.

Fried Mullet Indian Style

1 lb mullet
½ small onion, finely chopped
1 clove garlic
½ piece fresh ginger (1 inch long), finely chopped
¼ tsp ground turmeric
½ tsp chili powder
1 green Jalapeno, thinly sliced
¼ tsp cumin seeds
pinch of salt
lemon wedges, to serve
½ cup vegetable oil, for shallow frying

1. Except lemon and oil, blend all ingredients to a smooth paste.
2. With a knife, score both sides of the fish in a criss-cross design.
3. Rub the fish on both sides with the paste and let it rest for one hour.
4. Heat the oil on medium heat in a frying pan. When the oil is hot, fry the fish on both sides until golden brown.
5. Serve with lemon wedges.

Fried Mullet Thai Style

1 lb mullet
3 sliced Jalapeno peppers
1 thinly sliced onion
2 Tbsp fish sauce*
2 Tbsp flour
3 cups oil, for deep frying

1. With a knife, score both sides of the fish in a criss-cross design.
2. Roll the fish in flour to coat on both sides.
3. Heat the oil on medium heat in a frying pan. When the oil is hot, fry the fish until golden brown.
4. Serve the fish with a sauce made by combining onion, * fish sauce, Jalapeno peppers, and lime juice *OR* serve with a fish sauce of your choice, for example Tartar Sauce or Aioli Sauce.

Note: * commercially made and available in a supermarket.

Mullet, Stewed in Savory Tomato

2 pounds mullet
2 large onions, sliced
1 green pepper, finely minced
1 large garlic clove, cut up
4 large tomatoes or 3 cups strained tomato
1 tablespoon finely minced parsley
Salt, pepper and a little sugar
2 tablespoons butter
4 tablespoons flour
½ cup oil

1. Skin and cut the mullet into two-inch squares.
2. Simmer the tomato and season with salt, pepper and a little sugar. Place the pieces of fish in this to cook. Heat the oil and fry the onions, green pepper and garlic colorlessly, covering with a lid to keep them from browning. When tender, add to the tomato and fish, simmering all together.
3. Melt the butter, add the flour, stir and cook together; then add the roux to the tomato stew to thicken it. Taste to see if the seasoning is right; it should have a good, savory flavor.
4. Serve with mashed potatoes, boiled rice or spaghetti.

Ceviche

Ceviche has been one of South America's best kept secrets for centuries, but the growing Latino population have unveiled the shroud of mystery. Ceviche originates in Peru or Ecuador as both countries have a large variety of fish and shellfish. Fish spoils very rapidly and in the past there was no refrigeration. The people of that origin invented an ingenious method of preparing fish with lime juice that does not required cooking. Of course the fish was eaten on the same day. We may say that preparing "ceviche" is *cooking fish with lime juice*. The fish is marinated in lime juice for 3-4 hours altering the structure of the proteins in the fish, giving it the color and the texture of cooked fish.

There is no universal recipe and each country adds its own touch of individuality. Any fish or shellfish can be chosen and often fish is mixed with shrimp or squid. However, the main ingredients always remain the same: fish, lime juice, salt, pepper, and onions. Hot peppers, tomatoes, cilantro, and mangoes are often added. Ketchup, mayonnaise, vinegar, or Worcestershire Sauce may be added as well.

Safety considerations

Marinating fish in lime juice does not kill bacteria or parasites the way cooking does, so it is important to use the freshest fish possible. Mullet, like many other bottom feeding fish, may contain parasites that the lime juice will not kill. The available options are to steam the fish for 10 minutes or to freeze it for the required time at the prescribed temperature. The procedure is outlined in Chapter 3 - Safety Considerations. The advantage of steaming the fish first is that after 15 minutes of marinating time the fish can be served. When shrimp is added, it is advisable to buy fresh shrimp and then cook it for one minute only.

Mullet Ceviche

1 lb mullet trimmings (steamed fillets or whole fish)
½ lb fresh shrimp
1 medium red onion, sliced
2 lemons
1 jalapeno pepper, diced
1 mango (not too ripe), diced
2 Tbsp chopped cilantro
1 medium tomato, diced
¼ tsp salt
4 dashes Tabasco hot sauce

1. Steam mullet for 10 minutes. Scrape the flesh from the bones or cut fillets into ½" pieces.
2. Clean shrimp and boil for 1 minute in water. Dice into ½" pieces.
3. Squeeze the juice out of lemons.
4. Mix mullet with shrimp and add lemon juice.
5. Add diced mango, tomato, jalapeno, onion and cilantro.
6. Mix everything together and season with salt and Tabasco sauce.
7. Let ceviche stand for 15 minutes, then serve.

Photo 7.2 Ceviche.

Mullet Fish Cake - Traditional

Fish cakes are a classic dish that is found all over the world. It has been a way of using up leftovers that might otherwise be thrown away. You can use different types of fish, lean or fat, cooked or smoked, finely or coarsely chopped. Use milk or water; flour or boiled potatoes; eggs, egg whites, or no eggs; boil, fry or bake them, and add any other ingredients (shrimp, bacon, herbs, or spices) that you like.

Photo 7.3 Mullet fish cakes.

Cooked mullet trimmings, finely chopped	1 lb. (453 g)
Potatoes, cooked and mashed	1 lb. (453 g)
Small onion, finely chopped or grated	One (½ cup)
Butter	1 Tbsp
Heavy cream	¼ cup
White pepper	¼ tsp
Salt to taste	½ tsp
Parsley, chopped	¼ cup
Egg, beaten	1
Bread crumbs	as needed

1. Combine everything together and mix well.
2. Form into cakes, roll first in beaten egg, then in bread crumbs.
3. Fry in hot oil until golden brown on both sides.

Mullet Fish Cake - Indian Style

Cooked mullet trimmings, finely chopped	1 lb. (453 g)
Potatoes, cooked and mashed	1 lb. (453 g)
4 scallions, finely chopped	
2 green Jalapenos, finely chopped	
1 piece fresh ginger, finely chopped (2" long)	
fresh cilantro leaves, finely chopped	½ cup
parsley, chopped	¼ cup
salt and pepper to taste	
eggs	2
bread crumbs	as needed
vegetable oil, for shallow frying	
lemon wedges, to serve	

1. Combine everything together with *one* egg and mix well.
2. Form into cakes.
3. Dip cakes in beaten egg, then roll in bread crumbs.
4. Fry in hot oil until golden brown on both sides.
5. Serve with lemon wedges.

Spreads

Making mullet spread offers many advantages:
- You get more product when smoked mullet is made into a spread. It is after all easier to buy yogurt or cream cheese in a local supermarket, than to catch mullet.
- Mullet spreads taste great.
- It is a fancy product. Smoked fish spreads are very expensive so you end up with a product that you could be hesitant to buy.
- Spreads are easy to make.
- Spreads freeze well.

The following materials will make excellent spreads and dips:

Ingredients: butter, cream cheese, sour cream, plain yogurt, mayonnaise and avocado pulp. They can be added on their own or mixed together. It makes little difference whether you use plain yogurt or sour cream.

Flavorings: pepper, onion, garlic, cayenne, chives, parsley, dill, lime or lemon.

Smoked fish trimmings should account for at least 50% of the total ingredients, otherwise the flavor of smoked fish may be hard to sense. To a certain degree you can influence the color of a spread. For example in curry spread the color is yellowish due to the "turmeric" spice which is always present in curry mixtures. If you add more turmeric the color will be a stronger yellow. Paprika may be added as well and the color will be dark orange. Smoked paprika (pimento) has a deep red color so the color will be stronger. Another interesting spice is "annatto" which has a very dark red color. One teaspoon added to 8 oz mullet spread will introduce a pink tint in the spread. Avocado is of course green so the spread will appear greenish.

Food processors are of great help when making spreads. However, if you make a lot of spread, let's say 5 pounds, it is helpful to cut mullet trimmings into smaller pieces using a manual grinder. Use the smallest grinder plate you have. The grinder will do the job in a few minutes. Then you can finish the process using a food processor or mix everything together in a bowl.

Mullet Dip

Smoked mullet	8 oz. (225 g)
Sour cream	1 cup
Mayonnaise	½ cup
Scallions, finely chopped	1 Tbsp.
Lemon juice	1 Tbsp.
Tabasco sauce	3-4 drops
Worcestershire sauce	1/4 tsp.

Place smoked mullet trimmings, sour cream, mayonnaise and lemon juice in food processor and mix. Add other ingredients and process until smooth. Cover and refrigerate. Serve with potato chips or crackers.

Mullet Spread With Avocado

Smoked mullet	8 oz. (225 g)
Avocado	2 (about 400 g total)
Lemon juice	3 Tbsp.
Vegetable oil	1 Tbsp.
Double cream	2 Tbsp.
Garlic, smashed	1 clove
Salt and pepper to taste	

Place smoked mullet trimmings, lemon juice and oil in blender and mix. Add double cream, garlic, salt and pepper and mix again until smooth.

Mullet Soft Spread

Smoked mullet	8 oz. (225 g)
Sour cream	4 oz. (112 g)
Mayonnaise	2 Tbsp.
Heavy cream	2 Tbsp.
Lemon juice	1 Tbsp.
Onion powder	1 tsp.
Chives, finely chopped	1 Tbsp.
White pepper	½ tsp.
Salt	½ tsp.

Place smoked mullet trimmings, heavy cream and lemon juice in food processor and mix. Add sour cream, mayonnaise and all other ingredients and process until smooth.

Notes: chives may be replaced with dill. Take butter out of refrigerator and keep it for 1 hour at room temperature.

Mullet Curry Spread

Smoked mullet	8 oz. (225 g)
Lemon juice	2 Tbsp.
Plain yogurt	8 Tbsp. (2 oz., 56 g)
Mayonnaise	2 Tbsp.
Curry powder	1 tsp.

Place smoked mullet trimmings and lemon juice in food processor and mix. Add yogurt, mayonnaise, curry powder and process until smooth.

Mullet Pâté

Smoked mullet	8 oz. (225 g)
Softened butter	2 oz. (56 g)
Lemon juice	2 Tbsp.
Vegetable oil	1 Tbsp.
Cayenne	$\frac{1}{3}$ tsp.
Double cream	8 Tbsp. ($\frac{1}{4}$ cup)
Mayonnaise	2 Tbsp.
Egg white	1

Place smoked mullet trimmings, oil and lemon juice in food processor and chop in processor until smooth. Add double cream, mayonnaise, butter, cayenne and process again. In a separate bowl whip egg white. Add egg white and mix everything well again.

Notes: to soften butter take it out of refrigerator and leave for one hour at room temperature.

Mullet Spread With Cream Cheese

Smoked mullet	8 oz. (225 g)
Philadelphia cream cheese	4 oz. (113 g)
Softened butter	1 oz. (28 g)
Lemon juice	2 Tbsp.
Mayonnaise	4 Tbsp.
Sherry wine	1 Tbsp.
White pepper	½ tsp.
Nutmeg	⅓ tsp.

Place smoked mullet trimmings, lemon juice and sherry in blender and mix. Add cream cheese, butter, mayonnaise, pepper and nutmeg and mix again until smooth.

Mullet Spread With Horseradish

Smoked mullet	8 oz. (225 g)
Softened butter	2 oz. (56 g)
Lemon juice	2 Tbsp.
Plain yogurt	4 Tbsp.
Creamed horseradish	2 Tbsp.
Salt	½ tsp
White pepper	½ tsp

Place smoked mullet trimmings and lemon juice in food processor and mix. Add yogurt, butter, creamed horseradish and process again until smooth.

Notes: to soften butter take it out of refrigerator and leave for one hour at room temperature.

Mullet Guacamole Spread

Guacamole is a popular avocado based dip which originated in Mexico. Authentic guacamole is made with avocado, tomato, cumin, cilantro, and lime juice.

Photo 7.4 Guacamole spread.

Smoked mullet	8 oz (225 g)
Avocado	2 fruits (about 400 g total)
Lime or lemon juice	4 Tbsp.
Cilantro, chopped	2 Tbsp.
Medium Size Tomato (Roma), diced	1 tomato (80 g)
Ground cumin	⅓ tsp.
Medium onion, diced	1 (about 90 g)
Garlic clove, minced	1
Cayenne	⅓ tsp.
White pepper (to taste)	about ¼ tsp.
Salt (to taste)	about ¼ tsp.

1. Cut the avocados lengthways and scoop out avocado pulp.
2. Using food processor chop smoked mullet trimmings with lemon juice.
3. Add avocado pulp and all other ingredients. Process until smooth.

Sauces

There are some who complain that all fish taste the same. Smoked mullet is in a class by itself as it has a distinctive flavor, but it is unlikely that someone will eat smoked mullet all the time. A sauce provides an individual character to a steamed fish. Adding sauce to poached, fried or baked fish drastically changes its appearance and flavor and makes the meal more sophisticated. Place a piece of fried fish on a plate and it will remain just a piece of ordinary fried fish. Pour some sauce over it, add a sliced lemon, sprig of parsley and it becomes a dish. Although the idea of making sauce may seem intimidating to some, on the contrary, making sauces is fast and easy.

Sauce Making

You can make many sauces using one basic foundation sauce. This foundation sauce has been known as "drawn butter." It also goes by the name of "roux", which is basically thickening used for making soups, gravies and sauces.

- In making a sauce which contains egg yolks for thickening, the sauce must not boil after they are added or it will curdle. It must also be remembered that eggs will not thicken in a mixture unless the boiling point is nearly reached. The sauce must be carefully watched and at the first sign of boiling draw it aside where it cannot boil, then add the egg yolks and keep it where the temperature will be just under the boiling point. Remember that after the egg yolks are added, the sauce must never be left where it may boil again.
- In adding butter to a sauce, drop it in a small piece at a time, stirring each time until blended before adding another piece. If too much butter is added to a sauce all at once it might cause it to separate from the sauce, so for that reason it should be added gradually.
- Do not prepare sauces until you are ready to use them, but when they must be kept hot, place the saucepan in boiling water, where the sauce may be kept under the boiling point.
- Commercially made and available in a supermarket fish sauce may be used as a base in creating many of your own sauces.
- Tabasco pepper sauce or cayenne pepper can be added to any sauce to spice it up.

Chapter 7 - Cooking Mullet

Drawn Butter or Roux

3 Tbsp. butter (or oil)
2 Tbsp. flour
1 cup boiling water
Salt and pepper to taste

1. Melt *two* tablespoons butter, stir in the flour and allow to bubble up and cook together. *This roux is now ready for the addition of liquid*, which may be water, milk, fish stock, chicken stock, wine, etc.
2. Add the boiling water (or other liquid) and beat until smooth. Add the remaining *tablespoon* of butter, whisking until it is all worked in. Season with salt and pepper. This is a delightful sauce to serve with boiled fish, asparagus, or cauliflower *and can be used for making other sauces*:

Caper Sauce

Make Drawn Butter sauce and add a tablespoonful of capers to it.
Goes well with fish or boiled mutton.

Egg Sauce

Make Drawn Butter sauce and add two hard-boiled eggs, chopped fine.
Great for fish or poultry.

Hollandaise Sauce

Make Drawn Butter sauce and stir in additional butter, egg yolks and lemon juice to make a thick, yellow, custard like sauce with slight acidity.

Mustard Sauce

Make Drawn Butter and add mustard.

Parsley Sauce

Make Drawn Butter and add finely minced parsley.

Anchovy Sauce

Make Drawn Butter and add a 2 oz can of anchovies.

A fish sauce will have a better flavor if the *fish stock* is added to the *roux*. Make note that you would not add fish stock to let's say Hollandaise Sauce when serving it with chicken and broccoli, but it is fine to add fish stock when making Hollandaise Fish Sauce.

To make fish stock for sauces:

White fish trimmings, backbones of filleted fish, heads (gills removed), fins and tail pieces.

1 onion
1 celery
1 carrot
1 bay leaf
1 sprig of parsley
1 sprig of thyme

1. Place all ingredients in a pot and cover with cold water.
2. Bring to a boil, then simmer for one hour.
3. Filter through a fine strainer or a cheese cloth.

Note: fish stock freezes well.

Well Known Sauces

Aioli Sauce

2 cloves garlic
1 pinch salt
2 egg yolks
1 tablespoon lemon juice
1 cup oil (olive, vegetable or mixed)

1. Peel the garlic, put in a mortar and pestle with the salt and grind it into a paste.
2. In a mixing bowl whisk the egg yolks, lemon juice, and garlic mixture together until well combined.
3. Start adding the olive oil, drop by drop, whisking all the time. You can add it a bit faster as you go along, but the key to success is going slowly at the beginning.

Note: you can easily see that making Aioli is basically the same as making mayonnaise. So it should come as no surprise that the fastest way to make Aioli Sauce is to mix garlic paste with prepared mayonnaise. Aioli is a very popular sauce in France, Italy and in Spain.

Anchovy Sauce

3 Tbsp butter or oil
4 Tbsp flour
2 cups milk, or milk and fish stock, equal parts
One 2 oz. can anchovies
Salt and pepper to taste

1. Heat the oil or butter, stir in the flour, stir and allow to cook together.
2. Add all liquid all at once and whisk well with cook's whip until smooth.
3. Add anchovies and seasonings, mix until smooth.

Easy Anchovy Sauce

5 Tbsp anchovy paste or 4 anchovy fillets
1 cup mayonnaise or sour cream

Mix the anchovy paste with mayonnaise until smooth

Caper Sauce

2 cups milk, or milk and fish stock, equal parts
3 Tbsp oil
4 Tbsp flour
½ cup capers
1 tsp lemon juice
Salt and pepper

1. Warm up the milk (don't boil).
2. Heat the oil, stir in the flour and cook together, making roux.
3. Add the hot liquid, whisking until smooth.
4. Season with salt and pepper, adding capers and lemon juice.

Celery Cream Sauce

1 cup milk
½ cup cream
½ cup reduced celery water (saved after boiling celery)
1 Tbsp minced parsley
1 cup celery pulp (which has been boiled and rubbed through a sieve)
3 Tbsp oil
4 Tbsp flour
1 Tbsp butter
Salt and pepper

1. Heat the milk and celery water.
2. Heat the oil, stir in the flour and cook together, adding hot liquid and whisking until smooth.
3. Add the celery pulp, the cream, and the butter in small bits, stirring until all blended together.
4. Season with salt and pepper, adding the parsley just before serving.

Cucumber Sauce

1½ cups fish broth
½ cup cream
1 teaspoon lemon juice
Salt and pepper
3 tablespoons oil
4 tablespoons flour
1 tablespoon butter
1 cucumber, grated

1. Heat the stock, add the grated cucumber and simmer together.
2. Heat the oil, sift in the flour, stir and cook together, adding the hot liquid and whisking until smooth.
3. Strain, put on the fire again, add the cream and the butter in small pieces. Season.

Curry Sauce

1 cup milk
1 cup fish stock
1 teaspoon curry powder
2 teaspoons lemon juice
2 teaspoons onion juice
3 tablespoons oil
4 tablespoons flour
1 tablespoon butter
Salt and pepper

1. Heat the milk and fish stock.
2. Heat the oil, add the flour and the curry powder, stir and cook together, adding the hot liquid, whisking it smooth.
3. Add the seasonings.

Egg Sauce

2 cups milk
3 tablespoons oil
4 tablespoon flour
Salt, paprika
2 hard-boiled eggs, minced
2 teaspoons lemon juice
1 tablespoon butter

1. Scald the milk (don't boil).
2. Heat the oil, stir in the flour, cook together, add the hot milk all at once and whisk until very smooth.
3. Season and add the minced egg.

Hollandaise Sauce

½ cup butter
3 tablespoons flour
1 pint boiling water
3 egg yolks
Lemon juice to taste

1. Melt half the butter, sift in the flour, stir and cook together, adding a pint of boiling water all at once and whisking until very smooth.
2. Begin adding the butter, a small piece at a time, whisking each piece in before adding another, until all the butter is incorporated.
3. Draw aside from the fire and add the beaten egg yolks, just under the boiling point, whisking the sauce as it thickens. *Do not place it where it can boil again or the sauce will curdle.* Add lemon juice to taste.

Note: this sauce should be a thick, yellow sauce like a custard, with slight acidity, yet not sour. There are many other methods for making this sauce, but this is the most simple one.

Horseradish Sauce

1 cup milk
½ cup strong fish stock
2 teaspoons lemon juice
2 tablespoons grated horseradish
3 tablespoons oil
3 tablespoons flour
1 tablespoon butter
Salt and paprika

1. Heat the milk and fish stock.
2. Heat the oil and stir in the flour and cook together, adding the hot liquid all at once and whisking it until smooth.
3. Add horseradish and seasonings.

Horseradish Sauce, Cold

½ cup mayonnaise
2 tablespoons grated horseradish
1 cup whipped cream
Salt and pepper

Mix the ingredients in the order given and set on ice until ready to serve.

Mushroom Sauce

1 cup peeled fresh mushrooms, cut up in pieces
1½ cups milk
½ cup cream
1 egg-white, beaten stiff
Lemon juice to taste
3 tablespoons oil
4 tablespoons flour
2 tablespoons butter
Salt and pepper

1. Melt the butter and cook the mushrooms in it colorlessly.
2. Heat the milk.
3. Heat the oil, add the flour, stir and cook together, add the hot milk, whisking until smooth.
4. Add the cream and mushrooms, then season.
5. Beat the egg separately, combine with other ingredients and when about to serve the sauce add the egg, making a foamy sauce *which must not be boiled or it will curdle.*

Mustard Sauce

1 tablespoon mustard
1 tablespoon vinegar
1 pint fish stock
Salt and pepper
3 tablespoons oil
3 tablespoons flour
2 egg yolks
⅓ cup cream

1. Heat the fish stock.
2. Heat the oil, stir in the flour and cook together, adding the hot stock all at once and whisking until smooth.
3. Add the cream, then draw aside and add the egg yolks, under the boiling point, whisking them in as they thicken, but not allowing it to approach the boiling point again.
4. Make a paste of mustard and vinegar and add them to sauce. Season and serve.

Oyster Sauce

1 small can of oysters
1 cup milk
½ cup cream
1 teaspoon lemon juice
Salt and pepper
3 tablespoons oil
3 tablespoons flour
1 tablespoon butter

1. Open can of oysters and drain off the juice.
2. Heat the milk and oyster juice.
3. Heat the oil, sift in the flour, stir and cook together, add the hot liquid all at once, whisking until smooth.
4. Add the cream and the oysters, season to taste.

Parsley Cream Sauce

1½ cups milk
½ cup cream
2 tablespoons finely minced parsley
½ lemon juice
3 tablespoons oil
1 tablespoon butter
4 tablespoons flour
Salt and pepper

1. Heat the milk.
2. Heat the oil, stir in flour and cook together, add milk, whisking until smooth.
3. Add the cream, butter and seasonings.
4. When ready to serve, add the minced parsley.

Sauce Supreme

1 pint thick white sauce
1 pint chicken broth
1 cup cream
2 tablespoons butter
1 teaspoon lemon juice
Salt and pepper

1. Simmer the white sauce and chicken broth until reduced by half, be cautious in order to prevent its scorching as it thickens.
2. Add the cup of cream and the butter, whisking it in well, then season.

Note: chopped mushrooms may be added.

Tartar Sauce

1 cup oil
1 egg yolk
Juice ½ lemon
Salt and paprika
1 tablespoon finely minced dill pickle
1 tablespoon onion, finely minced
1 tablespoon parsley, finely minced
1 tablespoon minced capers

1. Put the egg yolk in bowl and begin to drop the oil, a drop at a time, whisking it in well, until the mixture begins to thicken; then add a little lemon juice and return to the oil again, which may be put in more rapidly, a teaspoon at a time, well beaten in until the amount is all used up.
2. Leave the sauce thick and add two tablespoons boiling water to finish the sauce and prevent it from oiling.
3. When cold add the chopped ingredients and cool. Refrigerate.
4. It may be freshened up for use again by adding half a spoon of lemon juice.

Note: making Tartar Sauce is similar to making the mayonnaise and the fastest way to make Tartar Sauce is to add 1 dozen of finely chopped little pickles (gherkins or cornichons) to 1 cup of prepared mayonnaise. You may add one teaspoon of prepared horseradish if available.

Thick White Sauce

3 Tbsp butter or oil
4 Tbsp flour
1 cup milk, hot
¼ tsp salt

1. Melt the butter, stir in the flour, cook together.
2. Add the milk all at once and whisk until smooth.

Note: to make medium white sauce use 2 Tbsp butter (oil), 2 Tbsp flour and 1 cup milk. This sauce may be used with boiled lobster, sweetbreads, chicken cutlets, potatoes, turnips, cabbage, and other similar dishes.

Tomato Cream Sauce

1 cup tomato puree
1 cup milk
½ cup cream
Salt, pepper and a little sugar
3 tablespoons oil
4 tablespoons flour
1 garlic clove, thinly sliced

1. Heat the tomato puree.
2. Heat the cup of milk and cream.
3. Heat the oil, cook the garlic in it, stir in the flour, cook together, adding the hot milk and whisking until smooth.
4. Add the hot tomato and seasonings. This recipe may be doubled, and

what is left, with the addition of fish stock or milk, will make an excellent soup for the following day.

Tomato Curry Sauce

1 cup tomato puree
1 cup fish stock
1 tablespoon onion juice
Salt, pepper and a little sugar
3 tablespoons oil
3 tablespoons flour
2 teaspoons curry powder

1. Simmer the tomato puree and fish stock together.
2. Heat the oil, cook the garlic in it, add the flour and curry powder, stir and cook together; add this to the boiling tomato, whisking as it thickens, then season.

Note: you can make your own tomato puree, but it will be much faster to use canned tomato sauce.

To make tomato puree:

½ gallon fresh sliced tomato or 2 large cans
2 large onions, sliced
2 bay leaves
2 garlic cloves, peeled and sliced
4 stalks celery
2 sprigs parsley
2 sprigs thyme
Salt, pepper and sugar to taste

1. Put all the ingredients in a saucepan and simmer gently for 1-2 hours.
2. Cool and strain it. Refrigerate.
3. This is now ready to use in all kinds of sauces calling for tomato.

Velote Sauce

½ cup white fish stock
2 Tbsp butter
2 Tbsp flour
½ cup cream

1. Melt the butter, add the flour, stir and cook together.
2. Add fish stock and slowly cook together for 10 minutes.
3. Warm up the cream and blend all together.

Note: Velote sauce is the foundation sauce for many other fish sauces.

Mayonnaise Sauce

Mayonnaise may be considered a type of a sauce. It is also a foundation base for creating more sauces, for example Tartar Sauce or Aioli Sauce. Mustard, horseradish, curry powder, tomato ketchup, anchovy paste can be added to mayonnaise to create new sauces.

½ cup mayonnaise
½ cup sour cream
1 Tbsp lemon juice
2 tsp curry powder

Blend all ingredients together.

Bechamel Sauce

This is a classic creamy white sauce which goes well with fish and vegetables.

1 onion
1 carrot
1 celery stick
½ tsp. black pepper corns
⅓ tsp. nutmeg or mace
1½ cup of milk
2 Tbsp. butter
⅓ cup flower
3 Tbsp cream
1 bay leaf
1 strip of lemon zest
Salt and pepper to taste

1. Chop onion, celery and carrot very finely. Add nutmeg, bay leaf, peppercorns, lemon zest and place all in a saucepan. Add milk and bring to a boil. Remove from stove, cover and let sit for 30 minutes.
2. Melt the butter in a saucepan, remove from heat and stir in the flour. Heat again and cook until the mixture thickens (1-2 minutes). This is known as making "roux."
3. Strain milk and vegetables through a fine strainer into a bowl.
4. Blend the milk gradually into the roux, stirring constantly. Bring to a boil and stir until the mixture thickens. Simmer gently additional 3 minutes.
5. Remove the source pan from heat. Season with salt and pepper and stir in the cream.

Note: when serving with fish half of the milk may be replaced with fish stock.

Cold Butter Sauces

Cold butter sauces are much easier to prepare than sauces. They can be prepared beforehand and kept in a refrigerator, unlike some sauces, for example Hollandaise, that does not freeze well. Then, at serving time, put a teaspoon of butter or as much as you desire on a hot fish. If the fish is cold, you can melt down the butter and poured it over the fish. When making a butter sauce, the first step is to cream the butter. This is a common procedure in baking. The difference is that we don't add sugar to butter when making fish sauces.

To cream butter:

Leave the cold butter sticks for one hour at room temperature. Put the butter in a bowl and beat it with a mixer or whisk manually.

Curry Butter

¼ cup butter
½ tsp (or to flavor) curry powder

Mix together and refrigerate.

Lemon Butter

4 Tbsp butter
2 tsp. lemon juice

Cream the butter, working in the lemon juice. Refrigerate.

Parsley Butter

½ cup butter
1 Tbsp lemon juice
1 Tbsp finely chopped parsley

Cream the butter, adding the lemon juice a little at a time and the parsley. Refrigerate.

Dill Butter

½ cup butter
1 Tbsp lemon juice
1 Tbsp finely chopped dill

Cream the butter, adding the lemon juice a little at a time and the dill. Refrigerate.

Horseradish Butter

½ cup butter
1 Tbsp prepared horseradish

Cream the butter, adding horseradish. Refrigerate.

Wasabi Butter

½ cup butter
1 tsp Wasabi
(Wasabi is a green Japanese horseradish).

Cream the butter, adding Wasabi. Refrigerate.

Garlic Butter

½ cup butter
2 Tbsp very finely chopped garlic
1 Tbsp lemon juice
Salt and pepper to taste

Cream the butter, adding the lemon juice a little at a time and the garlic. Refrigerate.

Ginger Butter

½ cup butter
2 Tbsp very finely chopped garlic
1 Tbsp lemon juice
1 tsp finely chopped fresh ginger
Salt and pepper to taste

Cream the butter, adding the lemon juice a little at a time and the garlic and ginger. Refrigerate.

Roe

The use of roe or spawn of fish, preserved by salting or pickling, is many centuries old. The name caviare is of Tartar origin and the preparation of sturgeon roe is a huge industry in Russia.

Italians prepare the roe of mullet as a table delicacy, calling it "botargo," derived from the Arabic word "butarih." Mullet roe sometimes called the poor man's caviar is a desired item in many countries: Greece (avgotaracho), Korea (myeongran), East Asia (karasumi), Spain (botarga), French (boutarque) and many more.

Mullet roe is yellow in color, very delicate and rather large compared to roe found in other fish. When cleaning the fish, save every particle of the roe, it may be parboiled in salted, slightly acidulated water (with vinegar or lemon juice) and then boiled around 8 minutes. Drain, and when cold pick out the pieces of membrane. Add a tablespoon of mayonnaise and mix to a paste. This will taste great on toast or in any kind of sandwich.

The milt, or buckroe (the part of the male fish which corresponds to the egg mass of the female) is as common as the female roe or eggs. It compares very favorably in food value with the roe and flesh of the fish. Mullet roe is exported in large numbers every year from Florida to Japan.

Large Roe, Cooked

Take one or two pair of large roe, of which the skin is unbroken, and dip each piece into heavily salted milk, then into finely sifted bread crumbs. Place in an oiled baking pan, sprinkle liberally with oil and bake in a very hot oven ten to fifteen minutes, according to the thickness of the roe.

Large Roe, with Bacon

Proceed the same as above, except to sprinkle the uncooked roe over with sliced bacon cut in small pieces, instead of with the oil. Remove to platter, garnish with sprigs of parsley and pieces of lemon and serve with tartar sauce.

Salad of Fish Roe

If any of the larger roe is left, cut it in dice, mix with twice the amount of finely minced celery and mayonnaise. Season with salt and plenty of lemon juice. Dust on top with paprika.

Small Pieces of Roe

Small roe, two to three inches long by one in width, have been pronounced as delicately flavored as the finest fried oysters. Several at a time may be dipped into the salted milk, dripped a moment, and then into finely sifted bread crumbs, arranged side by side in an oiled baking pan, sprinkled over with oil and baked in a hot oven about eight minutes. Arrange in center of platter with a border of parsley or celery leaves for a garnish and serve with tartar sauce.

Creamed Roe on Toast

Parboil in salted, acidulated water ten minutes, drain, and when cold cut into pieces. Make a white sauce by heating two tablespoons of oil, mixing with it two tablespoons of flour to each cup of milk. Season with salt, pepper, lemon juice, Worcestershire Sauce, mushroom, tomato ketchup or any preferred seasoning. Add the pieces of roe, and when heated through serve on piece of toast.

Scalloped Roe and Oysters

1 cup parboiled roe, picked free from skin
1 cup oysters
2 tablespoons oil or butter
3 tablespoons flour
1 cup milk (may be canned milk, diluted)
1 teaspoon tomato ketchup
Salt and pepper
Lemon juice

Heat the oil, add the flour, stir into a roux, add the hot milk. Heat the cup of oysters until edges curl, strain off the oyster liquor, add it to the white sauce, add the oysters, the pieces of roe and the seasonings. Blend well together. Put in individual ramekins or baking dish. Sprinkle over with bread crumbs which have been mixed with a little oil and salt, or a potato border may be piped with a pastry bag around the edge, with crumbs in the center. Bake ten minutes until crumbs are browned.

Flounder or Sole Roe, Creamed with Green Peas

1 cup roe, cut in pieces, parboiled and free from skin
1 cup green peas
3 tablespoons oil or butter
3 tablespoons flour
1 cup milk
1/3 cup cream
1/2 teaspoon Worcestershire Sauce
1 teaspoon lemon juice
1 teaspoon tomato ketchup
Salt and pepper

Heat the milk and cream. Melt the butter, sift in the flour, add the hot milk and cream, stirring well until very smooth. Add the pieces of roe, add the cup of green peas, season to taste and serve on pieces of toast, or in individual ramekins.

Creamed Roe, with Shrimps

1 cup parboiled roe, free from skin and cut in pieces
1 cup shrimp meat, fresh or canned, cut in pieces
4 tablespoons flour
4 tablespoons oil or butter
2 cups milk
2 teaspoons anchovy essence
1 teaspoon lemon juice
Salt and pepper

Put the milk on to heat. In another saucepan heat the oil or butter. Sift in the flour, stir together, add the hot milk, whipping together until very smooth. Add the roe and the shrimps, season with the anchovy essence, which will color it slightly pink, and the lemon juice, salt and pepper. Serve on toast.

Sandwich Filling of Very Small, or Broken Roe

1/2 cup broken parboiled roe, picked free from skin and mashed to paste
1 tablespoon mayonnaise
1 small pickle, chopped very fine

Boil the roe in salted, acidulated water ten minutes. Allow to cool, pick free from all skin and mash to a paste with a wooden spoon. Mix with mayonnaise and add very finely chopped pickle. Spread on thin slices of buttered bread.

Mullet Milt

Take a pair of mullet milt, cut in two, lengthwise. The object in cutting thus is to prevent them from curling up when cooking. Then dip each piece into salted milk, then into fine bread crumbs, place on an oiled baking pan, sprinkle over with oil and bake in a very hot oven ten to twelve minutes, according to thickness. Garnish with parsley and pieces of lemon. Serve with tartar sauce.

Creamed Milt on Toast or in Ramekin

Parboil in salted and acidulated (with lemon juice or vinegar) water ten minutes. When cold take out skin and cut into cubes. Make a white sauce with two tablespoons of oil or butter and two tablespoons of flour to each cup of milk. Mix the white sauce and cut-up milt together and season with salt, pepper, lemon juice, Worcestershire Sauce and some tomato ketchup. Serve on pieces of toast which have been first dipped into boiling water, then buttered. Or it may be served in individual ramekins with a top dressing of oiled or buttered crumbs and browned in an oven ten minutes.

Index

A

alder 67
American mullet 7
astaxanthin 67

B

bacteria 29–34
bait 13
baking fish 51
bleeding 52
blood 35
boat 24
brine 46, 53
brine table 56
brine tester 55
brining time 58
brinometer 55
bucket 20
buckroe 113

C

canthaxanthin 67
carbon dioxide 12
cast net 14
  brail line 15
  cleaning 21
  hand line 15
  horn 15
  lead line 15
  mesh 15
  size 17–18
  storage 20
  throwing 24–28
caviar 113
ceviche 89
  mullet ceviche 90
cleaning mullet 35
  butterflied mullet 36–41
  kidney line 41
  scales 35
  skin 35
  split mullet 40
  stomach lining 41
  whole mullet 42–45
  without cutting 51
clostridium botulinum 32
cold smoking 63
  smoking 73
cooking fish 30
cooking mullet 81
  baked 83
  broiled 83
  cooking temperature 83
  deep fried 83
cooler 24, 34
cooling 76

D

detritus 7
dissolved oxygen 12
drum smoker 66
drying 69
dry mix 59

F

fat content 82
filleting 49–50
  rib cage 50
finger mullet 10
firewood 64
fish 7
  color 67
  immune system 29
fish eggs 10
fishermen 13
fish eyesight 19
fishing 19
  bait 13
  boat 24

bridge 20, 22
dock 20
night 19
obstructions 22
pier 22
rod 13
seawall 20, 22
fish markets 11
freezer 34
freezing 30–31

G

gills 51, 83
gizzard 9

H

hanging 69
hickory 67
hot smoking 63

I

ice 24, 48
internal temperature 76

J

jagging 14
Japan 10

K

kidney line 41

L

lime juice 89

M

making brine 55–57
marbling 81
microwave 31
milt 113
monofilament 19
mullet 7, 9

calories 82
catching 13
fat content 82
healthy food 81
myoglobin 67

O

oak 67
omega-3 82

P

packing fish 75
parasites 12, 32–33
　controlling 33
pellicle 59, 70
photosynthesis 12
polarized glasses 24

R

ramekin 114
recipes 84
　baked Garam Masala mullet fillets 85
　baked large mullet 84
　baked small mullet 84
　fried mullet Chinese style 86
　fried mullet curry 87
　fried mullet fillets 86
　fried mullet Indian style 87
　fried mullet Thai style 88
　fried small mullets or fillets of mullet 85
　mullet ceviche 90
　mullet fish cake - Indian style 92
　mullet fish cake - traditional 91
　mullet, stewed in savory tomato 88
red mullet 7
refrigerator 34
restrictions 13
rib cage 50
roe 10, 11, 113–116

Index 119

creamed milt on toast or in ramekin 116
creamed roe on toast 114
creamed roe, with shrimps 115
flounder or sole roe, creamed with green peas 115
large roe, cooked 113
large roe, with bacon 113
mullet roe 113
roe season 9, 10
salad of fish roe 114
salmon milt 116
sandwich filling of very small, or broken roe 115
scalloped roe and oysters 114
small pieces of roe 114
roe knife 11

S

safety considerations 29
  brining 34
  cleanliness 31
  cooking fish 30
  freezing 30–31
  pickling 34
  thawing 30–31
salinometer 55
salometer 55
salt 56, 59, 60
salting 29
sauces 98
  Aioli sauce 100
  anchovy sauce 101
  Bechamel sauce 110
  caper sauce 101
  celery cream sauce 101
  cold butter sauces 111
  cucumber sauce 102
  curry sauce 102
  drawn butter or Roux 99
  egg sauce 99, 103
  Hollandaise sauce 103
  horseradish sauce 104
  mayonnaise sauce 109
  mushroom sauce 104
  mustard sauce 105
  oyster sauce 105
  parsley cream sauce 106
  parsley sauce 99
  sauce supreme 106
  tartar sauce 106
  thick white sauce 107
  tomato cream sauce 107
  Velote sauce 109
scales 83
scaling 38
schooling fish 11
silver mullet 7–8
smoke generation 64
  barbecue starter 65
  hot plate 65
  sawdust 65
  wood 67
  wood chips 65
smokehouse 76
  concrete block 77
smokers 76–80
  drum smoker 66
smoke sticks 79
smoking 30
smoking fish 61
  cold smoking 63
  hot smoking 63
  reasons 61
  smoking 73
  what is smoking 62
snatching 13
spawn 9, 10
spores 32
spread 93
  mullet curry spread 95
  mullet dip 94
  mullet guacamole spread 97
  mullet pâté 95
  mullet soft spread 94

starburst 19
stomach lining 41
storing 76
striped mullet 7–8

T

thawing 30–31
tropical waters 12

W

water 9
  brackish 9
  freshwater 9
  salinity 9
  temperature 9
  tropical waters 12
wood chips 65

Also by Stanley and Adam Marianski

MEAT SMOKING AND SMOKEHOUSE DESIGN
STANLEY, ADAM AND ROBERT MARIANSKI

POLISH SAUSAGES AUTHENTIC RECIPES AND INSTRUCTIONS
STANLEY MARIANSKI, ADAM MARIANSKI, MIROSLAW GEBAROWSKI

In Meat Smoking & Smokehouse Design readers are provided with detailed information about how to:

- Apply cures and make brines.
- Smoke meats, poultry, game and fish.
- Barbecue meats and build barbecues.
- Create your own recipes without adding chemicals.
- Design and build your own smokehouse.

The book explains differences between grilling, barbecuing and smoking. There are extensive discussions of curing as well as the particulars about smoking sausages, meat, fish, poultry and wild game.

ISBN: 978-0-9824267-0-8

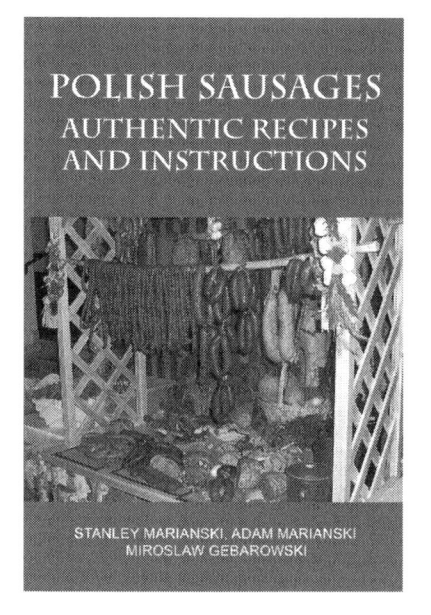

Most books on sausage making are filled with unknown quality recipes, this book is different, it contains carefully compiled government recipes that were used by Polish meat plants between 1950-1990. Those recipes were not written by restaurant cooks or college students running web sites, but by the best professionals in meat science the country had. The recipes presented in *Polish Sausages* come from those government manuals and they were never published before. These are recipes and production processes of the products that were really made by Polish meat plants and sold to the public. Most of those sausages are still made and sold in Poland.

ISBN: 978-0-9824267-2-2

Learn more at: **www.bookmagic.com**

Also by Stanley and Adam Marianski

There has been a need for a comprehensive one-volume reference on the manufacture of meats and sausages at home. ***Home Production of Quality Meats and Sausages*** bridges the gap between technical textbooks and the requirements of the typical hobbyist. Along with 172 recipes you will discover how to:
- Apply cures and make brines.
- Smoke meats, poultry, game and fish.
- Create your own recipes.
- Conform to U.S. Government standards.
- Make fresh, smoked, emulsified and fermented sausages along with head cheeses, blood and liver sausages.
- Make hams, bacons and loins.
- Make jerky, pemmican and more...

ISBN: 978-0-9824267-3-9

*In **The Art of Making Fermented Sausages*** readers are provided with detailed information about how to:
- Control meat acidity and removal of moisture.
- Choose proper temperatures for fermenting, smoking and drying.
- Understand and control fermentation process.
- Choose proper starter cultures and make traditional or fast-fermented products.
- Choose proper equipment, and much more...

ISBN: 978-0-9824267-1-5

Learn more at: **www.bookmagic.com**

Made in the USA
Columbia, SC
15 December 2020